# Crossroads after 50

# Crossroads after 50

## Improving choices in work and retirement

Donald Hirsch

The **Joseph Rowntree Foundation** has supported this project as part of its
programme of research and innovative development projects, which it hopes
will be of value to policy makers, practitioners and service users. The facts
presented and views expressed in this report are, however, those of the author
and not necessarily those of the Foundation.


Joseph Rowntree Foundation
The Homestead
40 Water End
York YO30 6WP
**Website**: www.jrf.org.uk

ISBN  1 85935 155 7 (paperback)
       1 85935 156 5 (pdf: available at www.jrf.org.uk)

A CIP catalogue record for this report is available from the British Library.

Designed by Adkins Design (www.adkinsdesign.co.uk)
Printed by Fretwells Ltd

Further copies of this report, or any other JRF publication, can be obtained
either from the JRF website (www.jrf.org.uk/bookshop/) or from our
distributor, York Publishing Services Ltd, 64 Hallfield Road, Layerthorpe, York
YO31 7ZQ (Tel: 01904 430033).

# Contents ▮

**Acknowledgements**                                                                                    **6**

1   Introduction: Towards a better understanding of transitions after 50      7
2   Older people in work                                                                           12
3   Older workers and their wider lives                                                    18
4   Decisions, choices and control                                                            22
5   Pathways in the transition from work to retirement                            29
6   Activities in early retirement                                                              33
7   Longer term financial futures                                                              36
8   Implications: Six key challenges for government and for society           41

**Appendix: Key findings from the Transitions After 50 research programme**      **47**

**Notes**                                                                                                  **58**

**Bibliography**                                                                                         **59**

# Acknowledgements

This report is an overview of what has been learned from the Joseph Rowntree Foundation's 'Transitions After 50' programme, which I have served as programme adviser. I am grateful to all of the researchers in this programme for their efforts to investigate this theme, not just in pursuit of their own research interests but also as a collaboration to produce a set of findings on common themes developed under the programme. The whole is certainly more than the sum of its parts: hence this report. Thanks to Anne Harrop, Sue Arthur and Sarah Vickerstaff for detailed comments on a draft of the report; to Mark Hinman for his help and support throughout; and to Christine Ashdown, Ruth Hancock and Patrick Grattan for being so supportive of the programme overall.

# 1 Introduction ■

## *Towards a better understanding of transitions after 50*

For much of the twentieth century, retirement appeared to be one of the great certainties of life, along with death and taxes. People progressed through their working lives with the firm expectation that, at a fixed age, they would abruptly stop work and enter a period of leisure supported by a pension. In practice, this was never a perfect idyll – many people, especially women, had irregular working lives, while inadequate pensions and poverty in old age remained widespread. Yet the idea of a fixed point of retirement for people in work, at age 60 or 65, at least created a stable set of aspirations for individuals, while making manpower planning more straightforward for employers.

In the twenty-first century, the ways in which people make transitions out of paid work in the later part of their lives will be much more heterogeneous. Already at the beginning of this century:

- Fewer than four in ten men are still working immediately before reaching the state pension age (compared with six in ten in 1980) (Cabinet Office 2000).

- Of people leaving full-time permanent jobs between 50 and state pension age, nearly as many enter part-time, temporary or self-employed work as stop working immediately.[1]

- While men (to a greater extent than women) are much more likely to leave work before state pension age than a generation ago, the government wants to encourage more to continue after this age, by improving incentives to defer state pension (DWP 2002).

- Ensuring adequate income in later life has become a far more complex process, with much more responsibility falling on the individual than in the initial Beveridge system. The basic state pension is no longer assumed to be enough to live on. Top-ups are provided by a complex array of means-tested credits, second state pensions, personal pensions and occupational pensions, the latter being subject to greater uncertainty as they become more commonly based on the value of invested contributions rather than a percentage of final salary. For each individual, lifetime earnings, savings rates and age at leaving work will combine with factors beyond their control – notably the state of the stock market and individual luck – in determining retirement income.

These changes are having profound effects on people's lives and have several underlying causes. One is to do with changes in employment, which offers fewer certainties than in the past; older workers have often suffered more than others from this as they are seen as dispensable when firms shed labour. Another is to do with the state's desire to diminish its commitment to look after people from 'cradle to grave', preferring to see its role for well-being as a shared duty in which individuals are also encouraged to look after themselves. A third factor, for some people, has been growing affluence: a longer period of retirement is one means of consuming increased wealth. But perhaps the most prominent factor influencing the ways in which we are now seeing the transition to retirement is demographic: the tension created by a combination of lengthening life expectancy and shortening work expectancy, resulting in higher dependency ratios. If this trend is sustained, people will eventually either have to accept lower relative incomes in later life or defer consumption of greater proportions of income in their working years, whether via private saving or public levy. As this trade-off manifests itself, choices available to individuals in terms of the timing and conditions of retirement will change.

Since the late 1990s, these factors have come together to make transitions to retirement an issue of serious concern to individuals, to the general public and to policy makers. There has been active public debate on the issue, and it has become a specific preoccupation within central government. In 1999–2000 the Prime Minister's Performance and Innovation Unit looked at 'active aging' in relation to policies across government departments, and published a report (Cabinet Office 2000) in which the Prime Minister committed his government to adopt actions and promote attitudes that help us as a society 'to recognise and use the huge talents of older people'. The creation in 2001 of the Department for Work and Pensions helped bring together thinking about relationships between what happens within and beyond work, exemplified by the inclusion in the 2002 pensions Green Paper of a chapter on 'extending opportunities for older workers' (DWP 2002).

The most powerful direction of response has been to challenge the 'writing off' of older workers and to look for ways in which they can be helped and encouraged to stay in paid work for longer. While this approach can be presented as improving opportunities for older people, it can also appear coercive, by making it harder for people to leave work early where they wish to do so. Thus while the desire to combat age discrimination commands widespread approval, strategies for lengthening the working life (for example, raising state pension age) are highly controversial.

Debates about these issues are rich in assumptions about what is best for people or about what they really want. Yet evidence about people's attitudes, behaviours and experiences in making early transitions out of working life has been sparse.[2] Over the past three years, the Joseph Rowntree Foundation has been strengthening this knowledge base, by commissioning a dozen research studies under the heading 'Transitions After 50' (see Box A).

The present report draws on that new pool of evidence to explore what we now know about people's lives during this period of transition. It argues that a debate revolving around whether people should be retiring earlier or later is misplaced. People in their fifties vary hugely in terms of their work situation, their expectations, their attitudes to work, their financial position, their health and their personal lives. Many difficulties that they encounter stem not from an inability to face up to the trade-off between income and leisure in later life, but from a lack of choice and control.

Thus the government is right to be searching, in its pensions Green Paper, for ways to 'extend opportunities' for older workers, as well as to ensure that they make more informed decisions (DWP 2002). But it would be a mistake to assume that with better maps and a more genuine choice of routes available, everybody would choose to travel down the same one. That is to say, in a world in which transitions after 50 worked smoothly, one 55-year-old might choose to retrain for a new career, another might work part-time, drawing part of a pension, while looking after an invalid parent or resting to preserve their own health, and a third might choose a relatively modest standard of living in order to be able to leave work entirely. The JRF's research shows that this diversity emanates not just from a spectrum of views on single factors such as how much money one needs to live on or satisfaction with one's present job, but on differences in people's wider approaches to work and to life in the context of different domestic circumstances. In this respect, public policy can help to create a more satisfactory set of options, but will not succeed if it tries to find a single solution appropriate for everyone.

Chapters 2–7 present the findings of the Foundation's 'Transitions After 50' programme, by looking at the various aspects of the transition process. In each case, after reviewing this evidence the chapter considers what policy levers are available to address the issues that arise. Chapter 8 then identifies six key challenges that governments and society need to address in order to develop more satisfactory approaches to this transition in today's world.

## Experiences during the transition: a framework for analysis

Transition from work to retirement is not always a clear, linear process. Some people in their fifties, for example, move in and out of different forms of work between having a stable career job and deciding to retire completely. Others, who lose their jobs and try unsuccessfully to re-enter the labour market, may find it hard to pinpoint a day on which they accept that they are permanently outside it. Still others take formal retirement but later re-enter work.

However, to analyse influences on how people experience this transition, it is helpful to look successively at issues arising before, during and after leaving work (see Figure 1). These form the basis of Chapters 2–7.

Figure 1 **Schematic model of transitions after 50**

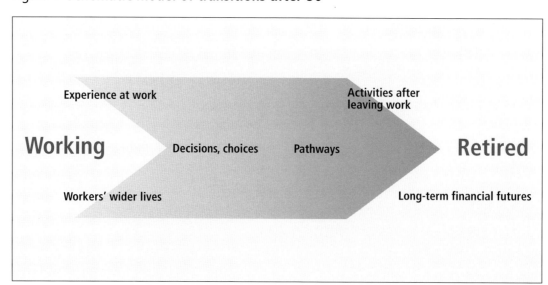

The context in which people approach the transition is determined by their experiences inside work (Chapter 2) and by what is happening in their wider lives (Chapter 3). During the transition itself, they are given varying amounts of choice over the timing and manner of their exit from work; Chapter 4 considers what kinds of choices are available and how people make decisions where such choices exist. Another aspect of the transition process is what pathways people take – and in particular whether they make an abrupt exit from a career job or 'bridge' the gap with other forms of work (Chapter 5). Once outside work, people develop new activities in various ways, and Chapter 6 considers how such activities relate to the process of leaving work. Financial factors are important throughout the transition, influencing, for example, how people regard their working lives, how they take decisions and the role of bridge jobs, and are considered throughout Chapters 2–6. However, one key question is the long-term effect that the nature and timing of the transition has on people's subsequent financial fortunes: this is considered separately in Chapter 7.

# ■ 2 Older people in work

*We need as a society to learn to encourage and use the huge talents of older people. I hope that our actions as Government will promote a wider change in attitudes.*
(Tony Blair, Foreword to *Winning the Generation Game,* Cabinet Office 2000)

*I must be honest with you, I've been dreading 50.*
(Tony Blair, *Saga Magazine,* April 2003)

## Issues

A cliché of our times is that older people represent a 'wasted resource' in the context of an ageing pool of labour. This is based on the assumption that older people's contribution at work is being undervalued at a time when, if only for demographic reasons, it will be needed more than ever. It is influenced partly by serious long-term shifts, in opposite directions, in the overall numbers and the participation rates of the over-fifties (see Box B). Yet it also reflects an underlying sense that as a society we have come to overvalue youth and some of its associated characteristics (such as vigour) at the expense of experience and the advantages that can bring. At work, this has undoubtedly contributed to early exit, whether voluntary by those who feel increasingly out of place as they get older or involuntary among those who lose their jobs and find it hard, because of their age, to find new employment.

The most tangible issue that these trends have raised in the past few years is that of age discrimination. Greater public and government acceptance of the existence and importance of this phenomenon contributed to Britain's decision to sign up to the EC Directive on Equal Treatment in Employment and Occupation, which obliges the government to legislate against age discrimination in employment by 2006. Other countries' experiences with such laws show that in themselves they can have at most a limited impact on deep-rooted attitudes and employment structures that disadvantage older people in work (Hornstein 2001). Yet age discrimination legislation can form the centrepiece of a more general attempt by government to promote positive attitudes and practices with respect to older workers, and signal that it takes the issue seriously. In the case of the UK, the commitment to legislation has been accompanied by the DWP's Age Positive Campaign, and a range of policies helping older people in the labour market. It has been supported by a range of initiatives from employers themselves, promoted in particular by the Employers' Forum on Age and by the Third Age Employment Network.

Yet government and employer responses to issues around older workers are only just beginning to address the fundamentals of older people's place in the workforce. In particular, a central dilemma encountered in other countries facing similar issues has been whether ending age discrimination in employment means being 'age-blind' and giving older people equal access to

### Labour supply and labour participation

As people born in the 'boomer' generation of the 1960s move through their forties and fifties during the first two decades of this century, the age profile of the working-age population will change quite markedly: the population aged between 50 and today's state pension age will grow by about two million while the 'working age' population below 50 falls by a similar amount. In addition, over two million extra women between 60 and 65 will be defined as 'working age', with the raising of the age at which they receive state pension. Yet at present, nearly a third of working-age people over 50 are not in jobs, a fall since the mid-1990s but still much higher for men than in 1980.

One way of describing the gradual but steady growth in the importance of older groups in the working-age population is as follows. For every 100 people in the labour market (working or seeking work):

- Approximately 21 are aged between 50 and state pension age; just one of these is unemployed, but a further eight people in this age group are outside the labour force.
- Based on current employment patterns, by 2021 about 26 workers will be aged over 50, with a further eleven in the age group[3] outside the labour force.
- A further six women will be aged between 60 and 65, and thus below the new state pension age; on current patterns only two will be working.
- The relative fall in the population of 25–45-year-olds is equivalent to losing about three or four workers, taking account of the participation rate of this age group.
- These population trends are complemented by, but much greater than, other downward pressures on the size of the labour market, such as increased study among young people. For example, if the percentage of people spending three years studying for a degree rose from a third to a half of the population, this would remove one further person from the 100-strong workforce.[4]

Note: These calculations do not take account of any effects of migration. If, for example, there is a net migration to the UK of younger adults, this would mitigate the rate of ageing of the workforce described above.

jobs by looking only at their capabilities and not at their chronological age. This is the dominant approach in the USA, where the older people's lobby asserts vociferously that there is no inherent difference between the capabilities of the old and the young. According to this view, where older workers lack necessary skills the right kind of training can help match them to available jobs. Alternatively, should efforts to improve older people's employment experiences centre not on matching workers to jobs but rather on matching jobs to workers? In some European countries, most notably Finland, efforts to integrate older people into employment have aimed to combine an improvement in occupational health with changes in the workplace. Finland's Programme on Ageing Workers (1998–2002) was aimed at improving attitudes to older workers and services available to them, as well as their preparedness for employment (Taylor 2002). This high-profile campaign has made Finnish employers aware of the need to be flexible in the way they structure work, both in terms of assigning occupational roles and in making flexible working hours available in cases where these are needed. This change has been prompted by a demographic crisis that has come earlier than in most countries.

## Evidence

There are many ways of looking at what is happening to older people in the labour market. Prior research has mapped demographic trends in labour force participation rates (for example, Campbell 1999; Gregg and Wadsworth 1998); explored how older people, males in particular, become detached from work (for example, Beatty and Fothergill 1999); tracked predictors of the timing of retirement (for example, Bardasi, Jenkins and Rigg 2000; Meghir and Whitehouse 1997); attempted to some extent to identify where there is age discrimination (for example, McKay and Middleton 1998) and looked to a limited degree at attitudes to early retirement within organisations (for example, Audit Commission 1997). This literature shows a range of factors compounding to make life in the labour market increasingly difficult for people as they grow older, sometimes starting from one's forties. However, it does relatively little to explore the attitudes and ambitions held by those affected by these factors, and how the influence of a primarily hostile work environment interacts with what is happening in people's lives. Nor does it give many clues about what kinds of policies might help older people to develop a more positive role within work organisations. The JRF programme therefore focused in particular on attitudes, to older workers' roles and to how they might develop, held by those workers themselves, by their employers and by their co-workers. (The scale of the programme did not allow a thorough survey of these issues, rather, a highly selective set of studies looked at aspects of work that might help illuminate more general points.)

A study on older nurses and how they fare in the NHS, while not seeking to be representative of older workers as a whole, was powerfully illustrative of the difficulties that many such workers find themselves in, and of the way in which their needs can be almost completely neglected (Watson et al. 2003). The facts are stark. The NHS faces an acute crisis in the recruitment of nurses. The proportion of nurses under 30 fell by more than half in the 1990s, while the number of nurses approaching 50 is growing faster than among any other age group. As they grow older, the pressures that have caused many nurses to retire from the NHS relatively early will come to bear on this cohort. Yet the study found that employing organisations are making no concerted attempt to adopt policies directed specifically at older nurses, either in terms of making working life better adapted to the needs of nurses in their fifties or by helping people of this age range return to practice after a career break.

In both cases, some fairly obvious options are available – such as redeployment to less physically demanding jobs, specific training in new technology and procedures, and options to downshift without compromising pension rights. Yet the system seems paralysed to the point of folly – a term defined by Barbara Tuchman (1985), in her historical masterpiece *March of Folly* as 'the pursuit of policies contrary to one's own interests, despite the availability of feasible alternatives'. The nurses study portrays an apparent march by the NHS towards an ever more severe staffing crisis, despite the available alternative of nurturing an already-trained pool of older labour.

To what extent is this kind of folly being repeated in various forms in other sectors of the employment market? Much is being done by some innovative employers, encouraged by campaigns run by organisations such as the Employers Forum on Age and the Third Age Employment Network. Yet in other cases, even where employers recognise in principle that they will need to make better use of older workers, they march ahead with policies that do little or nothing to reverse the neglect of this group. Overall, evaluation of the government Code of Practice on Age Diversity in Employment showed that awareness of issues around age has remained low, with most employers having few or no specific policies to address it (DWP 2001). While employers are reluctant to admit to treating older and younger workers differently, one of the strongest continuing prejudices revealed in this evaluation is that younger people are more worth training than older ones because they will remain in the workforce longer. In fact, given the higher rate of job change among younger workers (over fifties have on average been in their job nearly twice as long as those age 25–49), the expected future years of retention of an employee with an individual firm can actually be higher for older workers, giving greater opportunity to reap the fruit of a training investment.

An optimistic interpretation of the limited change so far in attitudes to older workers is that there is always a time-lag between the recognition that new attitudes are needed and their translation into practice – as has certainly been the case with gender diversity in many occupations. The case for age diversity has only very recently become widely acknowledged.

Another key factor in this kind of change lies in the ways in which employers manage personnel and the timing of their retirement, and how they manage the expectations of workers towards this transition. There is a sense in which the use of early retirement as a managerial tool in the 1980s and 1990s caused organisations as a whole to lose control of the retirement process. Local managers used mainly voluntary redundancy packages to shed labour where necessary with a minimum of friction; early retirement on favourable terms became an expectation among older worker; while younger workers saw those in their fifties as having a limited 'shelf-life'.

A study at the University of Kent on current trends in organisations shows that such a process is starting to reverse. Companies are trying to regain control of the retirement process, and to dampen the expectation of early retirement. Where they send out strong new signals, the attitudes and culture of the workplace in this respect appears to be transforming remarkably fast, with people expecting to work longer and realising that early exit on attractive terms is no longer likely.[5] This does not mean that there has been a complete reversal, from employers trying to get rid of older workers, to the opposite extreme of turning down all requests for early retirement. Rather, the Kent research indicates that employing organisations want to retain *flexibility* to offer early retirement as a means of reducing headcount or shifting particular employees. Final decisions about retirement are still largely at the discretion of the employing organisation, and depend to a great extent on the individual case. Indeed, the study illustrated how organisational demands can work either way, obliging people to retire either later or earlier than they would ideally like:

*"I would retire this year if the organization would let me retire. As you
know with local government you can retire at any time onwards from 50 but
between 50 and 60 it has to be with management permission before you can
actually draw your pension. So I'm at the stage at the moment of saying
I would like to retire and the organization is at the stage of saying we want you to stay."*

*"Well that really wasn't a decision on my part at all. It's policy
to retire you at 61 and in actual fact I would have liked to have stayed
because I was on a good wage and I would have liked to have stayed on
perhaps another two or three years."*
(Interviewees, Vickerstaff et al., forthcoming 2004)

## Policy levers

In his review of older workers' policies in different countries, Taylor (2002) draws attention to a wide range of approaches that can make a difference to older workers' fortunes. Although it is in many cases too early to evaluate the effectiveness of these different approaches, observing policies around the world is useful in thinking about the multiple features of such responses, no one of which can solve all problems. In particular, one can distinguish policies that:

- Help individuals: 'Labour market' policies helping older people to obtain or retain work, including training and employment services.
- Give incentives: Financial carrots and sticks such as wage subsidies or changes in benefit and pension rules.
- Promote fairness: Measures that constrain or encourage employers to treat older people fairly – such as age discrimination legislation and the promotion of age diversity.
- Improve working life: Measures that make the workplace better suited to the needs of older people, for example, in terms of improving work-life balance, making down-shifting more worthwhile, or practices supporting occupational health.

The first three of these aims to improve older people's chances in today's working world. The fourth poses a more fundamental challenge, of how to organise work in a way that allows older people to play a full role. In the DWP's (2002) Green Paper on pensions, the chapter on 'Extending Opportunities for Older Workers' proposes policies largely in the first three categories. In particular, it proposes:

- 'a new package of more intensive back-to-work help for people age 50 and over', not excluding those drawing close to state pension age;
- reform in Incapacity Benefit to link it to more active help and financial incentives to return to work;
- more generous rewards for individuals deferring state pensions beyond 60/65, and raising the minimum age for taking private pensions, to 55; and
- measures to outlaw age discrimination by employers.

These measures, and the emphasis by the DWP's Age Positive Campaign on selection, promotion and training based on merit rather than age, are designed to help older workers function better in the labour market. But is there scope to go further and change the character of work to take account of older people's characteristics as workers? One government proposal that takes a step in this direction is to allow workers to draw part of their occupational pension while continuing to work part-time for the same employer. This will assist downshifting. However, in the UK we are still a long way from the philosophy in Finland that work needs to adapt to help older workers remain engaged and healthy. A first step in this direction would be to extend the notion of work-life balance to address the needs of older workers, not just parents (the latter is the only group mentioned in this respect in the pensions Green Paper). To do so requires an understanding of the wider lives of workers over 50 and is discussed in the following section.

# 3 Older workers and their wider lives

*"We hear an awful lot about the value of families, well then I think somebody should start recognising that if you value the family you should start giving that family the respect it deserves... I'm not talking about necessarily a nuclear family, I'm talking about a family with all that implies... the responsibility that we each have for one another as human beings."*
(Interviewee, Mooney and Statham 2002)

## Issues

Workers in their fifties and early sixties experience a wide range of circumstances in terms of family situation, health and responsibilities and interests outside work. It is no more possible to make generalisations about their 'needs' than for the working population as a whole. Nevertheless, a range of factors affect many workers' lives as they get older, and as the evidence in Chapter 4 shows, these can play a major role in decisions about leaving work. They include:

- Problems with health and fitness: Overall, people are living and staying healthy for longer, yet for a large minority, long-term health issues have a serious effect on their later working lives. One in seven people aged between 50 and state pension age is claiming Incapacity Benefit (compared with 1 in 20 aged 25–49), and this accounts for half of those in this age-range who are not working.[6]

- Caring responsibilities: The 2001 Census showed that more people in their fifties than in any other age group are unpaid carers – about one in five of the population of this age. In particular, many care for older relations and for grandchildren (one in three people are grandparents by 50). Such responsibilities tend to be more hidden and less recognised by employers and colleagues than care of dependent children, adding to the pressure of juggling work and other obligations.

- Family and community obligations: As people go through life, their perspectives and priorities change. In some cases, pursuing one's career may become less important in later life relative to other obligations such as community and family roles. Changes in family circumstances, such as a partner having health difficulties or retiring, can be an important influence. These factors do not mean that older workers are all less focused on work, or that they are less committed to their jobs, than younger ones. Indeed, some things that can happen later in working life – including marital separation and children leaving home – can potentially help to strengthen ties with the labour market (for example, separated women may need to build up their own pension). Moreover, where older workers feel valued, they can often manage to reconcile competing work and life priorities. On the other hand, where negative assumptions are made about older workers' competence or commitment, feeling undervalued at work can help increase the priority given to domestic concerns. Thus, personal and workplace factors can interact with each other.

'Age-blind' attitudes at work may help to avert a vicious circle in which older workers feel ill-regarded by their colleagues and superiors and their commitment to their job weakens. Yet this does not mean ignoring the kinds of pressures common in older workers' lives described above. It is possible for employers to think about how to respond to such factors where they arise, without making any specific assumptions about a worker on the basis of their age, any more than an employer offering generous maternity leave should assume that because a younger worker is female she will become pregnant.

## Evidence

Across the research on 'Transitions After 50' commissioned by JRF, a recurring theme is the interaction between experiences in the labour market and personal health. As will be seen in the next chapter, this plays an important part in the timing of stopping work for many people. This interaction is often more complex than someone developing a sudden illness that makes them unable to work. Sometimes the effect of long-term health problems can be influenced by what happens at work – most obviously by whether someone with a physical impairment can be transferred away from physically demanding tasks (see, for example, Watson et al. 2003), but also in relation to stress, which can be exacerbated by an unsympathetic employer. As noted by Arthur (2003) decisions about the implications of health difficulties for someone's future in employment depend not only on their own decisions and doctors' advice, but also on decisions by employers. Employers who value older workers sufficiently may look for ways of retaining them despite health difficulties.

These considerations about health and retirement raise in particular the question of personal control. Older workers may feel they are losing control of the timing and process of retirement transitions not only because of deteriorating health itself but because of the ways in which employers and the social security system respond to it:

> "So that's when I got a note – a paper from the DHS saying, you are unable to work, you don't need to send any more certificates in. That flabbergasted me. Because I've always worked. I wanted to work. It got me down did that...That were like someone hitting me across the face with a cold fish...I mean you can imagine getting that through the post. A hell of a shock. 'Cos I thought, I'll get better, I'll go back to work."
> (Male ex-lorry driver, left work aged 53, received disability benefits, Arthur 2003)

An important study in the 'Transitions After 50' programme provides new evidence of the relationship between caring over fifties and participation in the labour market (Mooney and Statham 2002). No widespread evidence was found of people giving up work to take on caring responsibilities. However, the report suggested that the main impact on older workers was the extra burdens and stresses created on them while they continued working. These stresses were less likely to have a negative impact on aspects of work than on life outside work (see Figure 2). In other words, people typically put their work and caring responsibilities first, and as a result their own personal lives and welfare can suffer.

Figure 2 **The impact of caring on working carers (% who cite various factors)**

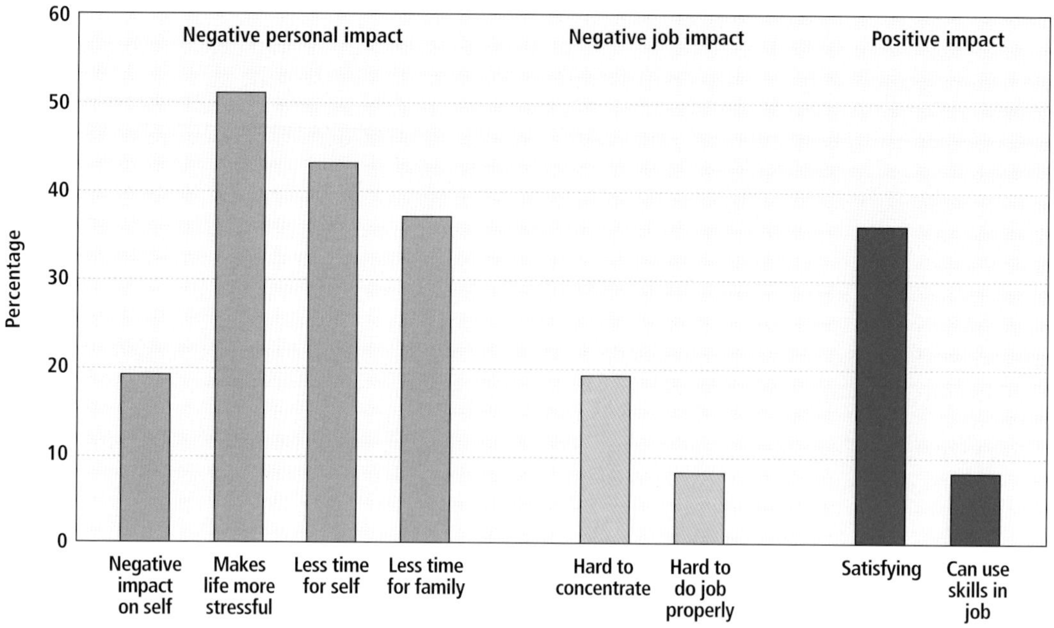

Source: Mooney and Statham 2002

The study showed a wide range of experiences in terms of the degree to which employers were sympathetic and accommodating to carers, but there was no evidence of systematic attempts to offer support through, for example, more flexible hours. Moreover, workers themselves hesitate to ask for allowances to be made, especially where they do not have a work culture in which colleagues are likely to sympathise:

*"Everyone's doing one and a half or two jobs. And so you know there's a constant feeling that you're not doing your job as well as you could anyway... you feel guilty about taking time off."*
(Male worker with caring responsibilities, Mooney and Statham 2002)

More broadly, the study concluded that there is a need for a change of culture and for a fundamental rethinking of the nature of work and care – not only within the workplace, but also in society more generally. Its authors argue for a culture which values caring and confers legitimacy on caring responsibilities. One of the workers interviewed for the study summed this up when she said:

*"The whole ethos of the workplace and the workforce has to change, and it has to come from the top."*
(Interviewee, Mooney and Statham 2002)

A caring responsibility is only one among many considerations that can affect the lives of older workers and potentially make them want to scale down their work commitments. Although the JRF research did not study domestic lives specifically, its findings point to evidence that women in particular can be affected by changing patterns at home, for example, when a partner retires. In general workers do not find it easy to 'downshift' within their jobs (see, for example, Vickerstaff et al. 2003; Watson et al. 2003). Two obstacles are employer approval and risk to pension entitlements.

## Policy levers

A key challenge to employers and to government in the coming years will be to apply the concept of 'work-life balance' to the context of older workers, not just to people with dependent children.

Such a task is not easy, since the needs and responsibilities of older workers outside work are not as readily defined or visible as parenthood. Even where someone is putting in a large amount of unpaid care of an elderly or disabled friend or relation, this is often a more private matter, to which the carer may not wish to draw attention. In the words of one carers' advocate:

> *"It is much harder to say to colleagues that you need to leave work early to change your father's incontinence pads than to pick your daughter up from school."*[7]

This suggests that the most effective way forward will not be to try to define what are 'legitimate' reasons for flexible working or time off, but rather to extend the availability and social acceptance of such flexibility for anyone who wishes to take it, as their self-evaluated needs change. Many of the companies with policies cited in the DTI's Work-Life Balance campaign (DTI 2003) offer flexible working options (such as banked hours) to all employees, not just parents. Yet that campaign remains highly focused on parents, as have been the most significant legislative provisions – notably the right to paternity leave, and the right for a parent of young children (under 6) to have a request for working part-time to be given due consideration. Thus the government could help lead the way to a wider interpretation of flexible working, by:

- Drawing greater attention to the needs of workers with changing life circumstances and caring responsibilities other than for dependent children, and giving greater priority to publicising examples of individuals with particular needs.

- Looking for ways of using legislation to this end. A first step would be to give all workers some form of right to have requests for part-time work or flexible hours duly considered.

- Considering more directly the ways in which income is supported in a transition between full-time work and full retirement that makes flexible pathways financially feasible. Such income issues are considered in Chapter 7.

# 4 Decisions, choices and control

*Probably less than a third of the fall in older people's employment has been voluntary.*
(Cabinet Office 2000: 9)

## Issues

At the heart of transitions after 50 are the ways in which people come to leave the labour market. This is determined by a combination of preferences and circumstances over which the individuals affected can have greater or lesser control. Two issues that arise, therefore, are:

- the factors that cause people to want to leave work at a particular stage of their lives or careers;

- the degree to which they are able to exercise choice, or to which the timing and manner of leaving the labour force are subject to factors beyond their control.

People's preferences can be looked at in terms of both 'push' and 'pull' factors. On the one hand, they may be disillusioned with work, find it hard to cope with its demands, or have health difficulties that cause them to retire. On the other, they may be attracted by the idea of retirement, with a chance to pursue their own interests, and believe that financial provision is sufficient to provide the lifestyle that they require. However, in many cases exit from work is not determined by these preferences alone, but wholly or partly by external factors, which limit the extent of individual choice.

The Performance and Innovation Unit report *Winning the Generation Game* (Cabinet Office 2000) estimated that at least two-thirds of the decline in older people's employment rates in the 1980s and 1990s was not due to people making a free choice to retire earlier because they could afford to. A high proportion of those not working are on Incapacity Benefit, and surveys show that where people retire earlier than expected this is more often instigated by the employer than the individual (Tanner 1997). Only a minority of those not working between 50 and state pension age live in households with occupational pensions, and the rest are twice as likely than average to be in the bottom fifth of the income distribution (Cabinet Office 2000).

The limited choice faced by many people leaving work early, especially those who drift out of the labour market via unemployment and Incapacity Benefit, suggests that a divide may be opening up between those who make satisfactory transitions to retirement which they are able to control, and those without control and less satisfactory outcomes. This is a key issue since 'two nations in early retirement' could be followed by two nations throughout retirement, with less fortunate groups ending up with lower pensions and less positive approaches to retirement than those able to control the process.

However, it would be misleading to suggest a simple dichotomy between voluntary and involuntary exit from work: the reality is often more complex. The most straightforward case of involuntary departure is where an employee is made compulsorily redundant, or where a worker without stable employment finds it impossible to remain established in work. Frequently, however, a limited amount of choice can interact with attitudes and preferences, for example, where voluntary redundancy is offered on terms that may not reoccur, and workers who do not feel strongly attached to their jobs take this opportunity to quit. In this case the decision to retire early, but not the exact timing of departure, is in the hands of the employee.

Even where people are able to make choices only within constrained circumstances, it is relevant to know what factors they take into account when deciding whether to leave work. For example, financial inducements to encourage people to stay longer in the labour market will only be effective to the extent that people who have some control over their labour market status are driven in their decision making by financial considerations.

## Evidence

A range of evidence on how people make decisions in making transitions out of work point to two overarching conclusions:

- More advantaged groups tend to enjoy greater choice and control over this process – although this takes the form of a range of experiences over a continuum of choice and control rather than a simple division into those who do and do not retire voluntarily.

- Financial considerations are important in making decisions, but often are not the driving factor but only a constraint determining whether or not one can afford to leave the labour market at a time when one would like to do so for reasons unrelated to money.

A useful way of thinking about the degree of control that individuals have over leaving a particular job and over the transition to retirement is illustrated by Arthur (2003) in Figure 3 overleaf and also by the examples in Box C. Looking first at the ways in which a specific job departure is made, the left diagram considers whether such a move is self-initiated and whether the timing is appropriate for the person involved. For people in quadrant A, the move is a positive, self-initiated decision. Yet even among those who decide to leave a job themselves, some are not ready to leave work entirely: those in quadrant B typically experience constrained circumstances such as health difficulties or a family obligation, which they may hope is temporary. On the other hand people in the lower half of the diagram (for example, quadrant D) have the decision forced upon them, for example, through redundancy or through compulsory ill-health retirement.

The right side of Figure 3 reflects the fact that retirement does not always come at a single clear point when people leave a job. In particular, people to the right of the diagram wind down from work over an extended period and may not be able to say precisely when they consider themselves 'retired'. A benign scenario, shown in quadrant 2, occurs where such a

Figure 3 **The early retirement process: dimensions of control and timing**

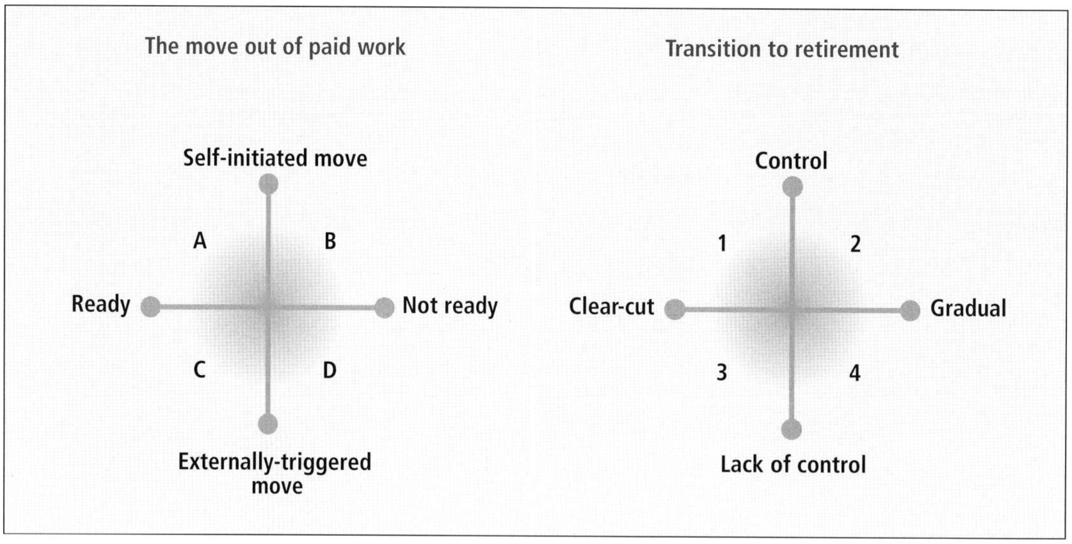

gradual wind down follows a conscious policy, for example, moving from full-time employment to full retirement via freelance work. Unfortunately, a more common pattern, especially for those with limited skills, is represented by quadrant 4: drifting gradually and unwillingly away from the labour market. In general, once someone in their fifties has not worked for at least two years, their chances of returning are extremely slim (Arthur 2003; Campbell 1999).

To what extent can people's positions on these axes be predicted by their general advantages and disadvantages, in terms of occupation and skill level. Certainly there is no automatic relationship, given that in many cases where firms have had to downsize, even privileged highly-paid workers have sometimes had limited control over the manner of their departure. However, the JRF's qualitative research evidence indicates that overall, disadvantaged groups have the worst outcomes in this respect.

Arthur (2003) found that three factors in particular interact to influence retirement pathways: people's work history and skills; their financial circumstances; and their health and disability status. These findings do not show that people with better prior circumstances always have greater control, but that they are better placed to deal with situations as they arise. For example, they are more able to negotiate better severance packages, and may be better positioned to find high quality 'bridge' jobs (see Chapter 5). Those with better financial situations may be less dependent on benefits, which can sometimes 'trap' people outside the labour market if they fear that doing a bit of work may compromise their ability to claim.

Similarly, among people who have left work, those who have experienced more satisfactory transitions tend to be financially more secure (Barnes et al. 2002). Those with the lowest levels of income are most likely to report that they do not have an opportunity to continue paid work, even though they want to.

These two qualitative studies also contain a rich array of descriptions of what criteria had been important to people when leaving work. The Arthur (2003) study sought principally to

## BOX C
## Examples of:

### Less control and choice

Robert Gray is 62, divorced, and worked most of his life as a bus driver. He moved to an office job within the bus company after he had a heart attack, but was made redundant in 1990. He then spent four years working as a supervisor for a local authority until he was 54; he was 'paid off' by the local authority when he became ill with bladder problems, and his heart condition worsened as a result of an operation. His doctor told him if he did not retire he would precipitate his death. He sometimes regrets listening to the doctor, as he would have liked to carry on working.

Mike Parker is 55 and stopped work three years ago when he was made redundant from his job as a trainer within the local council. He was given voluntary redundancy, but felt he had to take it because it might be his last opportunity to get a lump sum package. He had previously worked for the RAF, and then at a steelworks, before being made redundant in the early 1980s; he was then out of work for about ten years. His wife has not worked since having children, and now has arthritis and is a wheelchair user. When he stopped work three years ago, Mike would have liked to carry on working, but he has now begun spending more time caring for his disabled wife, and feels it would be difficult to leave her.

### More control and choice

Steven Marsden is 57 and left his mechanic job about two years ago. He had previously worked as a transport engineer, but had been made redundant twice during his career. He had always wanted to retire early, and decided to do so at the point when he felt he and his wife could manage financially; he was also starting to find his job too much effort, and wanted to spend more time with his wife. He has not worked since, and doesn't expect to.

Paul Clayton took early medical retirement just over a year ago, when he was 55. He worked as a senior manager in the engineering sector, and had always felt he would like to retire early. He has a degenerative illness, which he had been managing at work, but his employer put the decision about when to leave in his hands, and he picked a time when his wife was also leaving work, and there were company reorganisations. He is now doing some voluntary work, but does not expect to do any more paid work.

Source: Arthur 2003

look at financial transitions, yet found that, typically, money was not the key to when and why people retired, but rather an important factor that 'framed' decisions strongly influenced by personal and work-related motivations. It also found that financial calculations tended to look at feasibility of retiring in terms of immediate income relative to needs, rather than looking ahead to the situation once the state pension became payable. However, bringing the latter into consideration is unlikely to change many people's decisions since for the better-off the state pension is relatively unimportant, while lower-income workers are less likely to leave work early voluntarily.

The study by Barnes et al. (2002) set out specifically to investigate why a group of over-fifties who had left work before state pension age had done so, and found that:

- Many were influenced by the atmosphere of workplaces, in which they viewed age discrimination as a fact of life. One aspect was the way in which older workers were seen as the people who needed to go when decisions were taken to shed labour:

    *"Everyone who could jump, jumped, and those who didn't jump at that time then got shoved out."*

Others saw intensification of work as being the key problem – they had grown to hate their jobs, and by extension the whole labour market, in which there were seen as being few or no opportunities for starting afresh in anything other than low-grade employment.

- Deteriorating health (one's own or that of a family member) was a major reason for wanting to leave.

- People have often been influenced by a combination of factors including their personal circumstances, rather than by a single dominant factor. For example, a person dissatisfied with work who had a partner in poor health might find a financially favourable retirement 'package' particularly attractive. An important point to come out of this study was the significance of one's partner's situation to one's own decision making. For example, whether the partner is retired can make a difference – in either direction. On the one hand it can make retirement more attractive, where partners have plans to do things together. In other circumstances, however, having a partner in work can make retirement more financially feasible.

Overall, then, money is one among many influential factors. For some people if financial circumstances were different they would make different decisions – in particular a number of respondents said they would retire if they could afford to. Yet they cannot be considered independently of how people feel about work itself and about other things going on in their lives.

## Policy levers

The limited choice and control that many people have over their exit from work has deep underlying causes and no simple solutions. For those people who throughout their lives have had a relatively weak position in the labour market, this is simply one manifestation of their vulnerability. Only long-term policies to improve the quality of work and of people's skills – especially their adaptation skills – rather than measures directed specifically at older people, can ultimately start to reverse this.

However, these findings do carry some important messages for the government's agenda for improving opportunities for older workers (DWP 2002). They imply in particular that financial incentives to remain in work are unlikely, on their own, to be very effective. This is not to say that measures such as wage subsidies have no role to play, but that they need to be combined with other measures. This can apply to both 'sticks' and 'carrots'.

The government may be inclined to constrain the right of low-paid workers to make the choice of leaving work early, given that 'replacement' incomes on benefits can be close to 100 per cent and that the state therefore has to foot the bill for such a decision. This helps explain why it is particularly keen to encourage people on Incapacity Benefit and other benefits to consider returning to work. The government is less directly concerned about the choice of leaving work being exercised by those whose subsequent incomes come from non-public sources such as occupational pensions. Does this mean that a 'stick' of harsher benefit conditions could potentially be used to ensure that fewer low-income workers make an early exit? The biggest problem with this approach is that most exits by such workers are not led by considerations of what non-work income is available but by the interplay of labour market difficulties and other constraining factors in the lives of these workers. Thus under a harsher benefit regime many of them would leave work anyway, and simply end up worse off.

As for carrots, the Employment Credit giving a temporary subsidy to older people returning to work (and rolled into the Working Tax Credit in 2003) has been popular and successful, but has not obviously boosted employment rates. Although evaluation of the Credit has shown that a very high proportion of people remain in jobs once it runs out (Atkinson et al. 2003), a high proportion (around 90 per cent) also say that they would have taken the job regardless of the subsidy. This high 'deadweight' effect is consistent with the hypothesis that it is not principally money that determines whether older people work, but other factors including their perceptions of the workplace, their ability to obtain and retain employment and what is happening in their personal lives.

Thus non-financial support that helps to extend opportunities has to be at the centre of attempts to change the framework in which people over 50 make and execute decisions about work. The government has made considerable efforts through the New Deal to make specialist employment services available to older workers and those on disability-related benefits. Such services are welcome to many individuals, yet experience has shown consistently that once an older person has spent time outside the labour market their prospects of reintegrating are relatively slim. Measures that help address the underlying problem at its root, and prevent people dropping out of the labour market in the first place, may have a greater prospect of making a considerable difference to employment rates.

One response is a general assault on age discrimination, as described above. Yet there may also be a need for individuals to receive help and support in making their careers meaningful in the later part of their working lives. The evidence showing their disillusion and difficulty in engaging with work organisations supports this view. One approach is through better guidance. Careers and guidance services that have historically been heavily geared towards school leavers are only just beginning to reach older workers, for example, through Information, Advice and Guidance Partnerships. The greatest potential for such guidance is to build the capacity and confidence of older workers in managing their own careers. This can require relatively intensive assistance, which is perhaps most effectively provided through mutual self-help. For example, the Experience Works programme in the East Midlands has combined the promotion of the value of older workers among employers with courses and support groups that help these workers to develop their own skills, to project themselves, and thus to find an appropriate place in today's working world.

Thus governments need to think carefully about how best to develop a strategy of 'opportunities for older workers' that rebuilds engagement with the labour market among groups who are being pushed away from it by negative experiences of work, and pulled away from it by competing priorities in their lives. A traditional welfare system response, focusing on casualties already outside work and providing them with incentives and job-placement services is not likely to get very far. Only measures that aim to maintain motivation and capacity among older workers before they become disengaged, seeking to become their own agents in making the transition to retirement, will address the problem at its root. For this, support for locally-based, voluntary, networking initiatives of the kind that are already appearing in different parts of the country (for example, under the umbrella of the Third Age Employment Network), is likely to go further than advice provided by the employment service to people who have not worked for some time.

# 5 Pathways in the transition from work to retirement

*"I've played cricket for a number of years and I live very close to Broadstairs Cricket Club...they've got a vacancy for a groundsman coming up."* (Research scientist in the pharmaceutical industry, approaching retirement from career job, Vickerstaff et al., forthcoming)

## Issues

The manner of the transition from a working life to one of retirement has always raised some difficult issues for individuals. A 'traditional' retirement from a lifelong job at age 65, moving from a full-time job on a Friday, to a blank schedule on a Monday, leaves many people disoriented. Where such an abrupt or 'cliff-edge' transition is brought forward to, say, age 55 with a relatively unforeseen redundancy or early retirement package, this effect can be all the greater. Yet some forms of more 'gradual' transition to retirement can also be problematic – particularly where someone loses their job and continues to seek work, only to drift unwillingly into retirement for lack of opportunities. On the other hand, a more benign extended transition can involve 'bridge jobs' which enable people to continue working part-time, in a job with different responsibilities, in casual work or self-employment, or in a new career even after leaving their 'main' career job.

It would be a mistake to think that bridge jobs are the solution for everyone: for some people, an abrupt retirement at a particular age is an expectation and an aspiration. Yet the last two sections have highlighted the need for many older workers to balance work with changes in their personal lives, and to develop their work identities in later life in ways that make them feel they can make positive contributions. The availability of a range of opportunities to do different kinds of work during later-life transitions can thus help many people not to have to make a stark choice between either persevering with jobs that they no longer want to do, or quitting the workforce entirely.

## Evidence

A detailed analysis of the Labour Force Survey (Lissenburgh and Smeaton 2003) shows that the employment transitions of older workers are extremely varied. Substantial proportions of workers leaving permanent full-time employment after 50 do take up part-time, temporary and self-employed work. The survey found that 38 per cent of men and 55 per cent of women who were working in 'career' jobs a year previously, but not any more, were in such 'flexible' employment. Of these, the biggest group (nearly 46 per cent) was women leaving permanent full-time jobs who moved to part-time work. Additional evidence is provided by Phillipson (2002) who used longitudinal analysis from the British Household Panel Survey to show that a large minority of an age cohort combines part-time and full-time work. For example, among men aged 50–54, 21 per cent work both full- and part-time over the next eight years; for women aged 45–49 it is 26 per cent.

Such overall trends, however, mask a wide range of experiences in non-standard employment among different groups of workers. In some cases bridge employment can represent a positive step allowing one to move in new and interesting directions on one's own terms; in others it can simply be a downgrading of conditions.

A move to part-time work is particularly likely to lead to worse conditions, although in different ways for men and for women. Men are more likely to have lower satisfaction and job security, but similar rates of pay as they had experienced in full-time work; women more usually maintain job satisfaction and security, but experience lower pay.

Men tend to be happier with temporary jobs than women, probably because they are more often an extension of the work they did on a permanent basis.

A move to self-employment tends to offer the greatest satisfaction, with men and women who make this move finding that they have greater control over their working lives, even though they clearly operate under greater risks. However, the biggest divide is in the extent to which men and women manage to get established in self-employment – most over-fifties who do so after leaving employment are men, and those with higher qualifications and higher earnings are also more likely to make this shift.

Thus it is not bridge jobs *per se,* but the ability to use them in particular ways that can help produce more satisfactory transitions after 50. Barnes et al. (2002) provide some interesting insights into the role of paid work among older people no longer in full-time employment. They found that the ability to find such work relied to a considerable degree on skills and social networks gained from previous employment. Some people wanted to keep working as a way of continuing to feel involved; others were driven more by a financial imperative. Ironically, those who were most financially needy were least likely to find such work, whether because of lack of skills and networks or because of concerns about consequences for benefits.

Further evidence of the many different pathways that people can take is provided from research being completed at the University of Kent which looks at these issues from an organisational perspective (Vickerstaff et al. 2003). In two of the large employing organisations observed in this study, a substantial number of older workers taking early retirement or considering whether to do so were already in 'second careers' after retiring from previous 'career jobs'. This mirrors the American experience where many, male workers in particular, are forced or 'encouraged' out of their main career to take up lower paid, less skilled work in another sector. By contrast, in Sweden men are more likely to downshift within their main career organisation (Jacobs and Rein 1994).

The Kent study also gives considerable qualitative evidence that many older workers are keen to obtain bridge jobs but feel that the possibilities are limited – in particular in terms of opportunities to continue working in different roles for their own company. Consultancy with one's old employer seems largely restricted to people in higher-status jobs. Part-time opportunities are often not seen as an option, in some cases because of fears (sometimes misplaced) about the relationship between periods of part-time work and final pension level:

*"I think that is the irritant really at the moment, probably with most people, that in order to keep the final salary pension scheme you can't really do part-time working because you'll miss out on your pension."*

*"Well you get 1/60th of what is taken of your salary ... as far as I understand the more you work in the last year the more you're going to get as a final salary."*
(Interviewees, Vickerstaff et al., forthcoming 2004)

These comments from the Kent study illustrate how some workers appear to think that working, say, half-time in one's final year would halve one's pension, when in fact it would generally only halve the amount of eligible service accrued in that year. Employers have done little to correct such misapprehensions.

Thus, the extent to which UK employers allow, encourage and inform employees about the ways they can adjust work patterns can play a big role in framing the scope for finding appropriate transitional pathways. The evidence is mixed on employer behaviour with, for example, Mooney and Statham (2002) reporting that some working carers found their employers accommodating in this respect, and others less so. Constraints on pensions appear to inhibit the willingness of individuals to downshift in their first careers because their pension might be affected. Even though a move to part-time work in the same grade may have relatively little real impact on final pensions, this is not the case if one shifts to a different job with a lower salary as, for example, may be appropriate for some nurses in their final years in the profession (Watson et al. 2003).

## Policy levers

The most obvious and visible policy levers to make it easier for people to bridge satisfactorily the divide between full-time employment and full retirement regard the arrangements for taking pensions. Greater flexibility to combine work and pension income would make it financially feasible for more people to leave their jobs without retiring fully. A first step, long delayed by the Inland Revenue, was finally announced by the government in its pensions Green Paper: lifting the ban that prevents workers taking part of an occupational pension while working part-time for the same employer.

It would be possible to go much further. One possibility would be to impose new rules on final salary pension schemes to ensure that they are structured in ways that minimise the penalty for moving into lower-paid jobs (in terms of which earning years are taken into account when calculating final salary). A more adventurous and radical policy would actively encourage older workers to stay in work part-time – just as the tax credit system presently does for parents. This could involve a tax credit giving some matching support to those over 50 who have moved to part-time jobs.[8] Although as discussed earlier, financial incentives alone may not be enough to change behaviour, this kind of subsidy would help send a clear signal to employers and employees that the government is encouraging those who downshift as an alternative to drawing a full pension.

However, reducing the cost and increasing the incentive of taking up bridge jobs will not be of much use to those who lack opportunities to take them up. Much is in the hands of employers, in terms of the extent to which they are willing to use older people's talents more imaginatively. Most of the evidence shows that employers are at best 'permissive' of worker requests to move from their career jobs, rather than actively promoting such opportunities. Another crucial factor for employers is how they deal with labour downsizing, and in particular whether they are able to find ways of retaining the experience and talent of the older workforce without necessarily keeping everyone on full time. Government can work closely with employers and their organisations to encourage such new modes of behaviour.

At the same time, the agenda for lifelong learning needs to include the development of new skills among older workers to adapt to new roles. 'Mid-life should be a time of opportunity during which people have the choice to launch a new stage in their working lives', suggests the Third Age Employment Network in a report (Grattan 2003) that argues for much better guidance and learning opportunities at this stage.

This applies in particular to learning for self-employment, where that is a relevant possibility. For example, in the DTI's policies promoting entrepreneurship and social enterprise, the considerable potential of older workers leaving career employment needs to be taken into account. The evidence shows, not surprisingly, that so far professional and managerial workers, especially men, have been the most successful in bringing their talents and experience to market by becoming self-employed. Other groups need to be helped in similar directions.

The extent to which employers facilitate bridge jobs is also linked to their policies and attitudes towards older workers and their capacities. In particular, are they interested in retaining the contribution of workers with limitations linked to health or disability? To do so may mean thinking imaginatively about how to structure work, not always according to a 'mainstream' model of full-time employment at fixed hours. The government and voluntary sector have been active in promoting 'intermediate' labour markets in the form of supported employment for people who have spent time out of work. However, public sector organisations such as the NHS could think much more constructively about how to create changing roles for existing older employees whose capacities are changing, and so improve retention.

# 6 Activities in early retirement

*"You've got certain skills – you really ought to try and put something back into society."*

*"What I think of as a really luxurious day is not having to go out all day."*

*"I've always loved working with children."*

*"I like it very very quiet...too much of anything I don't like."*

(People who have left paid work early, Barnes et al. 2002)

## Issues

To what extent do people who leave the workforce early, often still fit and capable of a wide range of productive activities, put their efforts into active unpaid work within their communities? Society does not have a very clear set of expectations of this group. Some people see retirement as synonymous with leisure, in terms of relaxing and pursuing one's own interests without particular obligations to others. Others see later life as an opportunity to get involved with things that one does not have time for when one is in paid work. The present government sees older people as a valuable resource and is trying to encourage more people to 'put something back' into their local communities.

It would be risky to attempt to 'tap' this resource in an apparently 'exploitative' way, that takes for granted the unpaid contributions of people who in many cases have painful recent memories of being edged or forced out of paid work. Rather, an opportunity to participate actively in society needs to be seen as something that can potentially benefit the participant as well as society. For some people outside paid work, such participation may not be of interest; for others, however, lifting barriers to participation may be of considerable benefit. If it helps people rediscover a meaning and a purpose in their lives, this benefit is potentially at least as important as paid work.

The literature review carried out at the start of the 'Transitions After 50' programme (Hirsch 2000) noted a striking decline in volunteering rates among people in their fifties and early sixties. This appears odd in view of the declining employment rates of this age group, although less so to the extent that people in their fifties act as a 'pivot generation' in various informal activities, especially family care, which are not counted as 'volunteering' (see Mooney and Statham 2002, and Chapter 3 above). It is not easy to develop an overall characterisation of what people in their fifties are doing with their time, because of the heterogeneity of the population and of the types of activity (paid work, unpaid volunteering, informal care, leisure, etc.) in which they engage.

## Evidence

A team from the Policy Studies Institute adopted an innovative methodology to analyse what people are doing with their lives after leaving paid work between 50 and state pension age (Barnes et al. 2002). Rather than investigating who is taking part in particular activities, such as volunteering or caring, the study started with individuals, seeking out people in particular areas who were willing to report on their experiences and expectations. The findings of this qualitative study are not able to quantify across the population how much people are doing of each type of activity, but rather help describe the range of experiences encountered by this group.

As the quotes at the beginning of this chapter illustrate, experiences and expectations vary widely, from those who see retirement as a time for leisure and rest to those determined to get heavily involved in their communities. Activities noted in the study included voluntary work, learning activities, domestic work, caring for family members, helping out friends and neighbours, and leisure pursuits. The most significant findings of this study concerned not the overall incidence of these activities but the importance of an individual's circumstances in determining the extent to which they could benefit from each of them. In particular, people's health, income and family circumstances were important in how they spent their time in retirement. Those who were better off found it easier to achieve a high level of participation. So, it appears, did those who had had positive experiences of work and of leaving work: those who freely chose to retire tended to have higher levels of income and more options open to them.

A further study (Maria Power, forthcoming), looking at the experience of older volunteers and views of the professionals who organise them, confirms that the impetus for volunteering draws  heavily on the individual's own background. In fact, it finds that older volunteers today tend to have a long-standing ethos of helping and getting involved, rather than typically being people who have come to such activities later in life. In particular, people now entering their fifties are the generation born in the relatively affluent period in the second half of the twentieth century, with a greater sense of good-fortune than their parents and more of a sense of wanting to 'give something back'. The study also noted a strong influence of religious faith as a background to why many people volunteered during this part of their lives.

However, even though many older volunteers have been engaged in such activities throughout their lives, the nature of the activities often changes in later life. The Power study found a tendency for people to move from volunteering based around children's schools and related community groups, to more 'caring and helping' roles, sometimes linked with family obligations and at other times with the much wider world. For example, one woman, who with her husband had been helping a girl in Nepal financially when they were busy working, now wanted to go to Nepal to volunteer with the same organisation.

Both of the above studies noted an important element in the thinking of older volunteers: they were often quite particular and even demanding about what they wanted to do – about what activities they would find worthwhile. They were not simply willing to put themselves in the hands of a community coordinator and say 'how can I be useful?'

Thus the picture seems to be of a mainly well-off, committed corps of older volunteers who know what they want out of volunteering. Less advantaged groups are volunteering less, perhaps partly because they do not have the contacts and know-how to get what they want from such experiences – although they are certainly heavily involved in less 'formal' forms of activity such as helping family and neighbours.

## Policy levers

The big gap in policies to stimulate and enable people to volunteer remains the difficulty in drawing in less advantaged groups in the population. This research has not found any magic key to unlocking the potential of such groups. However, it has provided the following information about key elements in any strategy to draw them in:

- For people leaving work, positive experiences at the time of exit are likely to help improve the quality of life in early retirement, if only by maintaining people's self-esteem. Successful strategies for bridge employment can help avoid the dislocation involved in abrupt departure from work, and create greater continuity.

- Stronger support for volunteers would send out signals that they are valued by society, which can be particularly important to worse-off groups who fear financial exploitation and are not used to 'working for nothing'. In the USA, small stipends have helped serve this purpose for many years, and this is a possibility that could usefully be looked at more closely in the UK.

- The more that activities can be projected in terms of *mutual* help across a community, the more widely they are likely to appeal to people across the social spectrum. Volunteering as 'helping the worse off' may seem of limited relevance to people who feel badly off themselves. On the other hand, models such as 'time banks' are founded on the principle that everyone can make a contribution (in terms of their own time), as well as being able to draw something out.

# 7 Longer term financial futures

*"We thought that basically we would be quite well off, comfortable, hopefully, on one salary as opposed to the two salaries that were coming in...I think we felt very much that it was an experiment to start with and it would take us a year or two to work out exactly how much we did need and whether the calculations had been right or not – and if they weren't, we would have to draw our horns in."*
(Female ex-teacher, left work aged 53, received pension lump sum plus income of £7,000 a year)

*"What's your pension going to be? You don't know. I've sent off for a [frozen occupational] pension prediction but it's still not real...Until you've got it in your pocket you don't really know what it is."*
(Male ex-engineer, left work aged 61, no retirement income of own at the time, wife had pension lump sum of £46,000 plus annual income of £15,000)

(Arthur 2003)

## Issues

In a 'perfect' economic world, early retirement would involve a conscious trade-off between income and leisure time. In practice, this often does not occur, for a variety of reasons.

One is uncertainty and lack of information: people simply do not always know what the long-term effect of retiring early will be on their living standards in later life. Once the decision is taken, and ties with the labour market thus weakened, it may be too late to adjust the balance of work and leisure in the light of changing circumstances.

A second reason is that such a financial trade-off may not always exist in reality. For example, someone who is offered an attractive early retirement package several years before pension age may be better off accepting it than rejecting it and being made redundant on worse terms two years later.

Third, many people leave work in highly constrained circumstances, being obliged to retire either because they are made redundant and have limited further options in the labour market, or because personal circumstances, such as ill health, leave them with no real choice.

Yet even if this trade-off is not recognised at key decision points, the consequences of early retirement can be potentially severe. This may be more so in the next 20 years than in the past 20, given that superannuation funds are no longer as healthy as in the years when they were used as an easy way to pay off surplus labour in periods of downsizing. Where people have significantly lower pensions than they would otherwise have had, as a result of missing say the last five years of work before pensionable age, they may have to live with the resulting hardship over the next 30 or 40 years.

For people on low incomes, many of whom rely primarily on state benefits, will fewer years of earning pension entitlements matter? The answer depends to a considerable extent on the role of means-tested benefits, which is changing. Until 2003, for people with pensions below the minimum income guarantee, who claimed this benefit, every extra pound of pension entitlement resulted in a £1 withdrawal of benefit, and thus made them no better off. Recent increases in this benefit relative to the retirement pension have accentuated this poverty trap. However, with the new Pension Credit, even though more people will be means-tested, the marginal withdrawal rate will fall from 100 per cent to 40 per cent, meaning that any reduction in state or private pension entitlements related to early withdrawal from work will have at least some negative impact on living standards. Moreover, between a quarter and a third of pensioners entitled to a means-tested top-up are estimated not to claim it, with over 60 per cent of non-claimants entitled to at least £10 a week.[9]

These considerations raise issues both of the relationship between early retirement and future living standards, and the transparency of that relationship for those having to take decisions affecting their futures. Does the timing of workforce exit contribute to poverty, and to what extent are people able to plan for their financial futures?

## Evidence

The research on income consequences of early retirement shows no clear and automatic link between leaving work early and risking low income in later life. It does show, however, that for some groups such a link exists. Yet the complexity and frequent changes in the situation facing pensioners makes it difficult both for researchers to identify clear consequences and for older workers to make sound judgements in their decision making.

Bardasi and Jenkins (2002) set out to consider the effect of early workforce exit, alongside other aspects of work history, on the risk of low income in later life. Their analysis of results from the British Household Panel Survey found, unsurprisingly, that your occupation is a much more important factor than your retirement age in predicting whether you have low income in retirement. The total number of years worked has a significant predictive effect in this respect for some occupations but not others, and the same is true for the number of years that one works in one's fifties. Specifically, men working in clerical jobs, in craft occupations, in personal and protective services, and in sales occupations have increased chances of suffering low incomes in later life if they work fewer than five years in their fifties. An important finding of this research is that for women this is not a major factor. Their chances of having to survive on a low income in later life are primarily related to the incomes, if any, of others in their household. Those without partners have the highest risk.

Thus, while the timing of retirement can matter, it is only one among many factors, and it cannot be assumed that everyone who leaves work early will suffer low living standards. This was underlined by another piece of research by Meadows (2002) who used results from the Family Resources Survey to analyse the incomes of retired people according to whether they had left work before state pension age. Again, there was no relationship in the case of women but men, particularly those now in their seventies and eighties, are on average better off if they retired earlier than otherwise. This may be due partly to the generous packages that many early retirees were able to access 10 or 20 years ago, but could also reflect a 'compositional' effect. People who retire early on lower incomes often do so in poor health, and have low life expectancy. Those who retired early who are still living in their seventies and eighties are thus disproportionately the better off.

These pieces of evidence are, of course, retrospective. They measure current income levels of people who left the workforce some years ago, but will people leaving the workforce today, or in years to come, have the same experience? The end of the 1980s–1990s bull stock market, the shift from final salary-based to contribution-based company pension schemes and changing demography may all combine to increase the penalty to individuals of leaving work early. They all make it less likely that workers will be able to leave in, say, their mid fifties and receive pensions that are little different from those that they would have received had they stayed on longer. When these factors are combined with the end of means-testing with 100 per cent withdrawal, researchers must conclude that the past is not necessarily a guide to the future.

Individuals, too, have learned to conclude this, both with respect to the performance of the stock market and their private pensions and with respect to public pension provision. This real uncertainty, in combination with limitations in many people's knowledge and understanding of financial matters, makes long-term planning difficult.

The research certainly shows that many people's financial literacy and access to information is limited. For example, the study on nurses by Watson et al. found that they received very little systematic information about work and retirement options:

> Information came from informal advice from colleagues in canteens, by word of mouth or, in one case by 'one little form that kept getting photocopied'
> (Watson et al. 2003)

Arthur (2003) found that many people do have access to a considerable amount of financial information when considering or preparing for retirement, but only in certain contexts. Advice is most commonly available to people in certain occupations, especially professional ones, where employers provide it. They receive most information and advice when deciding how to structure an early retirement package, rather than more generally when deciding about when to leave work. At the time of leaving work calculating their private pension income is relatively straightforward, but they find it harder to foresee how this will interact with benefit entitlements, either in the immediate future or once they get the state pension. An interesting finding from Arthur's research is that on leaving work before state pension age, the people who are most vulnerable to income drops are not the very poorest groups (whose income in work may not be much above, say, Incapacity Benefit), but those on modest incomes who risk sinking into poverty as a result of premature departure from the workforce.

Finally, it is worth noting that while financial planning is not always the deciding factor in determining early exit from the workforce, people outside work in their fifties and early sixties do consider money an important feature in their lives. Participants in focus groups discussing experience and expectations at this stage of their lives (Barnes et al. 2002) identified money as the most critical element in older people's contentment and well-being. Financial security reduced stress and was seen as something that would them give greater choice over their lives in retirement:

> *"Financial security means I can be in control, as I have been the rest of my life. I don't want handouts, like the £200 for fuel. I want to be independent, not told what to do."*
> (Hackney Focus Group)

As part of this desire for control, participants wanted the benefits system to become more flexible, making it easier for people to take on part-time or occasional work.

## Policy levers

It is beyond the scope of this report to suggest measures that will provide everyone with financial security in retirement. However, the experiences of people during transitions after 50 should help frame the development of such measures, by taking into account the following:

- *The need for much greater transparency.* At present, it is extremely difficult if not impossible for someone leaving the workforce early to predict with any reliability what this decision will mean for their income 10 or 20 years hence. The complex array of public provision for pensions and means-tested income top-ups contributes greatly to this confusion, and makes it worse for people on lower incomes than for those relying principally on private/occupational pensions. In developing more durable, trusted and stable forms of income provision in later life, governments need to make a priority of informing future recipients about what they can expect to receive under different scenarios. There is also a need for wider and more individually tailored forms of financial advice than is presently available for many people trying to make strategic decisions about exit from work. Although government is right to encourage employers to provide pre-retirement planning, it would also be helpful for many people to have access to courses that are detached from the immediate situation of one's present job.

- *The need for more systematic protection during the transition itself.* Many people in their fifties and sixties find themselves, in practice, obliged to retire early for lack of work opportunities. Many give up looking for work after a period. At present, the main state benefit available to support them is Incapacity Benefit (IB), paid to over a million people between 50 and state pension age, representing half of those not working. The fact that claiming rates for this benefit are much higher in areas where jobs are more scarce illustrates that people's physical capacities interact with the level of demand to influence prospects in the labour market. Over the long term, it may be more productive to develop an explicit early pension for people outside the labour market for a long period in this age group, rather than requiring them to demonstrate medically-defined incapacity. Ideally, such a pension would work on an insurance principle, replacing a proportion of lost earnings for displaced workers, and thus help smooth out financial transitions not just for the very poorest workers who benefit from the present flat rate.

- *The fact that people may combine working and claiming benefits or pensions for considerable periods during the transition.* The benefits system continues to assume a dichotomy between those inside and outside the labour market, although the new Working Tax Credit does help people with interrupted work patterns to claim supplements to their earnings based on annual income. People receiving Incapacity Benefit, on the other hand, continue to worry that if they work they will risk losing entitlement. The government is right to try to change this: ideally, benefits should be a protective cushion for periods outside work rather than an impediment to working at all, particularly for those who may only be able to do so sporadically.

- *The considerable differences between the experiences of men and of women.* As the government's pensions Green Paper (DWP 2002) points out, women are the most likely to be underprovided for in terms of independent pension entitlements. This is particularly likely to lead to poverty among women without financial support from partners. For those with partners, decisions about work are often based on partners' situations, both financial and in terms of their health and employment status. Clearly one priority is to take steps to help women build up greater pension wealth of their own. This is likely to require, among other things, a better understanding among women of the importance of doing so, particularly in terms of the extent of their vulnerability in the event of being separated or widowed. At the same time, in shaping incentives to remain in work, the government needs to take into account the fact that financial carrots and sticks related to their own jobs will not always affect women's decision making, given the importance of various other criteria. Thus a general caution against introducing financial incentives that penalise workers for making early exit decisions that they will continue to make regardless of the incentive, applies in particular to the case of women.

# 8 Implications ■
## *Six key challenges for government and for society*

The evidence gathered by the JRF shows that many people making transitions after 50 are facing multiple pressures and have limited control of their lives. While a number of those interviewed in the course of this research expressed attitudes that were accepting of their situation, this should not lead us to underestimate the potential social harm that can occur as a result of inadequate opportunities at this stage of life, especially among already disadvantaged groups. In addition to the risk of material hardship in old age where people are unable to provide adequately for retirement, those experiencing untimely and unhappy dislocation from the labour market can suffer considerable psychological damage, entering retirement with low self-esteem that limits their capacity to attain their goals and play an active part in society during later life.

Government, employers and society in general are starting to wake up to these challenges. Yet the first steps being taken to meet them are tentative ones. Much remains ambiguous. Are we simply asking everyone to work longer? Should employers be discriminating 'positively' in favour of older workers? How should we be regarding the high rates of 'incapacity' among people in their fifties – as a medical or as an economic phenomenon, or an interaction between the two? While there are not always clear-cut answers to these questions, some clear priorities are suggested by the research reviewed above. These can be summarised as six challenges for government and for others in society, including employers, who make decisions affecting transitions after 50.

## 1 Improve choice and control for the 'have nots' in later working life

One common image of early exit from the labour force has been that of a male white-collar worker in stable employment tempted into early retirement when his company restructures. In practice, those with least control over their transition out of work, and at greatest risk of resulting hardship, fit a different pattern. Many come from manual occupations, sometimes with a sporadic employment history, often with no significant occupational pension, and quite frequently experiencing health difficulties in mid-life. One group, namely displaced male manual workers, has suffered particularly in areas where heavy industry has declined (Beatty and Fothergill 1999), but they are not the only ones who are vulnerable in today's labour market. Women who work intermittently and self-employed men without stable work, for example, are vulnerable not to a sudden lay-off but to a drying up of work opportunities linked to low local labour demand or to prejudice against hiring older workers. Compared with those leaving lifelong employment, they are much less likely to have an occupational pension to fall back on.

In a market economy there is no single straightforward way to improve the position of those in the weakest position in the labour market. So far, much government emphasis (under its welfare reform programme) has been on measures providing assistance and incentives for people who have spent a period out of work to re-enter employment. For the over fifties, these efforts have focused on the New Deal 50plus, combining the Employment Credit with practical help. However, it is widely acknowledged that, in light of the poor prospects of people in this age group once they have spent some time not working, a significant improvement in outcomes depends on improved rates of labour market retention rather than re-entry. This requires:

- New attitudes among employers towards older workers' value. The Government has made a major effort to promote these through its Age Positive Campaign, but it still has a long way to go, as shown in the Evaluation of its Code of Practice, DWP (2001).

- A concerted effort to improve personal development opportunities for less advantaged older workers, in ways that help them to remain in the labour market. This requires better access to training, education, guidance and advice. The PIU report, *Winning the Generation Game* (Cabinet Office 2000), recommended that such opportunities should be extended in various ways. For example, the Learning and Skills Council, should 'consider the needs of older workers as part of its overall strategy'. In its current Corporate Plan (Learning and Skills Council 2001), the LSC sets objectives and targets related to young people and to the literacy level of adults overall rather than specifically to older workers' needs. On the other hand, organisations such as the National Institute for Adult and Continuing Education (NIACE), through its 'Older and Bolder' campaign, have been vigorously promoting learning for older people. An ambitious effort to spread this approach across public learning providers and employers requires not just the inclusion of more older workers on particular courses, but an approach capable of addressing the wider development needs of individuals. This may, for example, mean helping them acquire the skills to become self-employed or negotiate a new relationship with an employer. Thus there is a particular need to extend local initiatives that give flexible support and guidance to older workers.

## 2 Fit jobs to older workers as well as older workers to jobs

A repeated theme among people interviewed in the JRF research is that as they get older they feel increasingly out of place in today's working world. In some cases, the solution is clearly better training, for example, in new ICT skills that have become essential to most workplaces. Yet it is difficult to conceive of training programmes that address, say, the feeling that work has become over-stressful and structured in a way more suitable to younger than to older adults. Enough of those leaving work early feel this way to raise some fundamental issues about how the world of work might change to become more attractive to an age group whose participation will be essential to economic success in years to come. A country such as Finland has been asking itself such questions because it believes that, demographically, it has no choice. Its conclusion has been that firms have to change in ways that promote occupational health and work-life balance to ensure that working remains an attractive option for longer than it has been for many workers in the recent past (see Taylor 2002).

What does it mean to fit jobs to older workers? The answer will vary according to the specific situation; the important thing is for employers to *consider* how to meet the changing needs and tap the evolving competencies of employees as they get older, rather than simply having a rigid formulation of a job's requirements. This may involve, for example:

- Looking for ways of shifting staff with manual duties to more administrative posts as part of their career development. An example is in nursing, where giving older staff the option of doing less heavy lifting is one way of improving retention of older workers (Watson et al. 2003).

- Restructuring job descriptions to create more opportunities for mentoring and other advisory tasks, potentially on a part-time or contracted out basis, which would allow older workers to use their experience without necessarily continuing to have executive responsibilities.

## 3 Create a new balance of priorities between working, living, health and well-being

As part of such an effort to retain older workers by changing their opportunities within the working world, there is a need to make work-life balance a serious priority beyond the context of families with children. As discussed in Chapter 4, this does not mean assuming that everyone over 50 is exhausted and needs to work part-time; rather it means giving more choice throughout working life, balancing commitments inside and outside of work. It also means taking occupational health, including psychological aspects, far more seriously than has hitherto been the case. This has been the approach in a number of North European countries, where deteriorating psychological health at work from age 40 is considered to be a central cause of the detachment of older workers from the labour market. Possible approaches to these issues include:

- Extending choice about flexible and part-time working hours to more workers. While attitudes in the UK towards part-time work have been relatively positive compared with other countries, the focus so far has been on women in certain occupations in which part-time working is dominant and on flexible arrangements for working parents. Extending rights and, potentially, some modest income top-ups to those working part-time at other stages of life would help promote part-time working as a socially acceptable option more generally.

- Giving greater public acknowledgement to the contribution made by carers of people other than dependent children, and their huge value to the economy. This needs to be reflected in greater support for their needs, particularly when they are working. For example, policies that improve the flexibility allowed to carers to take breaks from work and to receive training when they return would demonstrate that it is not just dependent children who provide a legitimate reason for spending time away from work.

- Giving a stronger priority to various aspects of long-term occupational health when making and enforcing health and safety legislation.

# 4 Make financial choices after 50 more transparent

The long-term financial implications to an individual of leaving the workforce prematurely remain shrouded in ambiguity and uncertainty, particularly for those with heavier dependence on state provision. A clearer picture of what it will mean not just for one's resources in the short-term but also for income beyond state pension age would help people to make informed choices.

A first step would be far clearer information about how much entitlement to state pension one has built up. The government is working to improve such transparency, and in doing so it needs to ensure that the full implications of working more years are made as clear as possible. This is not easy in the present complex system of interaction between means-tested and contribution-based income in retirement. However, as long as such systems exist, the government will need to consider carefully the following:

- How to present as clearly as possible a written pension entitlement statement which takes account of the effect of means-tested entitlements (a DWP pilot to give people statements of their public and employer entitlements has been encouraging, though more development work is needed).

- The provision or sponsorship of a basic advice service that allows an individual to have their full circumstances assessed.

Is transparency always a good thing? One form of transparency that could be seen as having had mixed results concerns the way in which employers run superannuation funds. The PIU Report *Winning the Generation Game* (Cabinet Office 2000) pointed to the fact that in the 1990s, managers making decisions about early retirement packages did not have to foot the true cost of shedding staff, which were hidden to the company as they were picked up by then well-endowed pension funds. Since that report, pension fund rules have been tightened, introducing a minimum Funding Requirement and the new accounting standard FRS17, both of which serve to make employers' pension liabilities and solvency more transparent. Employers have cited these changes as one factor causing a shift away from final salary schemes, which they say have become too expensive. Is there a risk therefore that if the cost to employers of using pension funds to restructure staffing becomes more transparent, they will simply worsen the terms of their pension schemes? While this argument may be tempting, commentators have suggested that transparency rules are simply an excuse by employers to do what they wanted to do anyway, in a much more difficult financial environment than existed five years ago (see Vickerstaff et al. 2003). Overall, it does not seem sustainable to run pension schemes on the basis of hiding information on the financial implications of decisions from organisations, managers and individuals.

## 5 Improve opportunities to build retirement income among people other than males in stable careers

A growth in the inequality of income among pensioners is due in large part to the very different opportunities that different groups have to build up retirement income. Only people in long-term stable jobs have hitherto been able to acquire occupational pensions yielding a substantial proportion of in-work earnings. Women who have interrupted work records, self-employed people and others without stable employment find it hard to build up their own private entitlements, and in some cases to make enough contributions even to receive the full state pension.

The Green Paper on pensions (DWP 2002) recognises the particular disadvantages faced by women, but proposes nothing that would change these fundamental difficulties. This could only be done by two types of long-term change: an improvement in people's work histories and changes in the generosity of the public pension system to people who have had limited opportunities to build up their pensions. Stakeholder pensions only help these groups by creating vehicles for them to make unsubsidised contributions to private pension schemes. This will not make a big difference to the incentive and ability of people on low incomes to build up adequate pensions. While it is much beyond the scope of this report to propose further reform in the pension system, any future reform should consider the particular need for assistance to people not in continuous stable employment.

One consideration would be the case for giving extra help and incentives for people with irregular work histories to build up pension rights after 50. Such incentives might help considerably in keeping more people in the workforce for longer. Despite the fact that, as this report has noted, financial incentives do not determine retirement behaviour, there is still potential for them to be an important influence for many people. In particular, women, who already experience a less sharp decline in employment rates between 50 and state pension age than men, might be more inclined to stay on if they thought that it could really make a difference to their pension. Some women interviewed in the research (for example, Watson et al. 2003) indicated that there was not much point in staying on to build up a pension as it was too late to do so. One possibility would be to allow people whose estimated pension entitlements fall below a particular level at the age of 50 to contribute thereafter to funds that are excluded from means-testing calculations when they are paid out.

## 6 Develop new modes of paid and unpaid work accessible later in life

For people in the last third of their lives in the twenty-first century, income will not be the only thing that is unequally distributed: potentially just as important will be inequalities in the opportunity to go on contributing to society and thus in underlying self-esteem. A professional worker who retires to become a self-employed consultant and sits on a board of governors will be better off in more than just money than a redundant manual worker who sits at home bored and depressed. A fundamental problem noted in this report is that in terms of paid bridge jobs and in terms of making contributions outside paid work, it is those who have had the most fulfilling work experience who once again seem to have the best opportunities.

A challenge for all of society is to become more inclusive in this respect. Just as employers need to learn better how to tap the skills of their own workers as they grow older, so communities need to become better at using the talents of a wide range of people once they have left career employment. One element of this in which the government can have influence concerns the benefit system: it needs to be made much clearer to people on benefits such as Incapacity Benefit that they can become actively involved in their communities without risking their benefit payments. At the same time, people with changing capacities as they grow older, including those who acquire disabilities, need to be helped to move into different kinds of employment, where necessary partly supported by public subsidy. The Disabled Person's Tax Credit has been a first step in this direction.

Yet while government can set down certain ground rules, ultimately a more inclusive range of opportunities will depend on the ways in which attitudes and organisations develop at a local level. So far, volunteering organisations have not been particularly good at reaching out to older people from working-class backgrounds. This suggests that new models of volunteering need to project models of mutual self-help that people from all backgrounds can relate to. It is beyond the scope of this report to design such models, but the findings reported here suggest that they need to be substantially different from those used in the past.

## Conclusion

This report has argued that transitions after 50 represent a crossroads from which different routes will suit different individuals, and that there is now a need to open up a better choice of directions. The government cannot control what happens to people at this stage of life, but has a number of levers at its disposal that can help improve opportunities. Employers and society generally can help to do so by changing their attitudes and regarding older people as a vital resource rather than an inconvenient burden.

While recognition of these arguments is growing, it could take some years for an ethos that reflects them to become ingrained into work and society. Legislation to outlaw age discrimination in employment, due to be implemented by 2006, will help accelerate this process. On the other hand, it could be slowed down if a conflict develops between a government appearing to tell everyone to work longer and individuals who want better choices and who fear an imposition of later retirement. Moreover, for many of those who have already left employment, welfare-type measures trying to urge them back are likely to lead to considerable frustration. For this reason, the main emphasis needs to be on developing better opportunities, flexibility and support for older people within the workplace. If workers can be helped to play a positive, though in some cases a changing, role in the labour market as they grow older, eventual transitions away from work should become smoother.

# Appendix ■

*Key findings from the Transitions
After 50 research programme*

This appendix includes the key findings of each research project:

Age discrimination legislation: Choices for the UK          48
Work history and income in later life                       49
Early retirement and income in late life                    50
Fxperiences and expectations of people leaving paid work after 50   51
Public policy initiatives for older workers                 52
Transitions from work to retirement: Developing a new social contract   53
The role of flexible employment for older workers           54
Nurses over 50: Options, decisions and outcomes             55
Informal care and work after 50                             56
The financial circumstances of early retirement             57

The findings are published in full as four-page summaries by the Joseph Rowntree Foundation, and can be found on the JRF website (http://www.jrf.org.uk/knowledge/findings/).

All reports in the Transitions After 50 series are published by The Policy Press in association with JRF and are available from Marston Book Services on 01235 465500 (p&p £2.75, plus 50p for every extra publication).

Two further publications from the programme (Power, and Vickerstaff et al.) will be published in 2004.

# Age discrimination legislation: Choices for the UK

The United Kingdom has committed itself to legislate against age discrimination in employment for the first time, by signing up to a recent European Commission Directive. A number of other countries already have such legislation. This study looked at what can be learned from those countries' experiences and analysed the options for the UK in designing age discrimination laws. The study identified legislation against age discrimination in employment in 13 countries, and looked in detail at three (Australia, Canada and the United States) where it has been established for some time. It found:

- Evidence of the overall effect of such legislation is in most cases weak. However:
  - Legislation has had a positive effect on employment rates of older workers in the United States. This is mostly due to them leaving jobs at a later age, rather than to more of them being hired.
  - Employer behaviour has changed in countries with legislation, to the extent that explicit discrimination, especially in recruitment, has reduced. However, society's and employers' attitudes to older workers do not yet appear to have shifted as much as towards groups such as women and people from minority ethnic communities, where legislative protection has, generally, operated for longer.
  - Forbidding employers to set mandatory retirement ages may have made them a bit less likely to hire older workers, but there is no evidence that this has been a major disincentive.

- The international experience points to the importance of some key choices about how to design legislation in the UK. In particular, legislators must decide:
  - Whether to deal with both age and other forms of discrimination in a single law and agency. To do so would show that age discrimination is viewed seriously, but age also risks taking a 'back seat' in a single agency.
  - What powers to vest in the commission that will enforce the legislation: in particular, whether to give it proactive powers of investigation and regulation.
  - Whether to permit employers to set mandatory retirement ages.
  - What to exempt from the legislation. Human rights considerations must be balanced with economic efficiency and other objectives; but too many exemptions tend to discredit anti-discrimination laws.

Published July 2001
(*Findings* reference number 711)

The full report, **Outlawing age discrimination: Foreign lessons, UK choices** edited by Zmira Hornstein, is published for the Foundation by The Policy Press (ISBN 1 86134 354 X, price £14.95).

# Work history and income in later life

As working lives shorten and retirement lengthens, there is concern over whether individuals make adequate provision to avoid poverty in old age. A study by Elena Bardasi and Stephen P. Jenkins of the Institute for Social and Economic Research examined the relationship between the risk of having a low income in later life and people's lifetime employment history. The study, based on data from the British Household Panel Survey (BHPS), found that:

- Although employment rates of older men fell sharply in the 1980s, they stabilised during the 1990s. Older women's employment rates increased during the 1990s.
- In the period immediately before retirement, people start to work less and earn less on average, but income still falls sharply in the year of retirement.
- Spending more years in paid work in total between the ages of 20 and 60 did not necessarily lower the risk of having a low income when aged 60+. Instead, the effect depended on the occupational group involved. A reduction in low-income risk was associated with more years of paid work for men in professional, and personal and protective services occupations, and for women in managerial, professional, technical and clerical occupations.
- Holding the number of years spent in an occupation constant, the risk of having a low income when aged 60+ varied according to occupational group. For men, those groups with small low-income risks were professional and clerical occupations, whereas, for women, they were professional, clerical and managerial occupations.
- Working fewer than five years between the ages of 50 and 60 raised the chance of having a low income in later life for men who had spent more of their working life in clerical, craft, personal and protective services, and sales occupations. By contrast, for women, low labour market participation between the ages of 50 and 60 had little association with the risk of having a low income when aged 60+.
- Household type and marital status were more important determinants of low income in later life for women than for men. Women aged 60+ living without a partner had a substantially higher risk of low income than women aged 60+ living with a partner, even if they had worked for much of their life.

Published April 2002
(*Findings* reference number 482)

The full report, **Income in later life: Work history matters** by Elena Bardasi and Stephen P. Jenkins, is published for the Foundation by The Policy Press (ISBN 1 86134 401 5, price £12.95).

## Early retirement and income in later life

There is growing concern about the tendency for retirement from paid employment to take place before state pension age. One uncertainty is whether people who retire early have sufficient financial resources to support themselves through possibly thirty or more years of retirement. This report compares the financial position of people in the current pensioner population who retired early with their counterparts who retired at state pension age.

It uses statistical methods to compare the two groups, who are matched in terms of key factors known to influence retirement, including gender, age group, housing wealth, ownership of financial assets, age at leaving full-time education and health status. The report suggests that planned voluntary early retirement may not be as disadvantageous to an individual's financial position in later old age as many fear.

Published July 2002
(No *Findings* was published for this report)

---

The full report, **Early retirement and income in later life** by Pamela Meadows, is published for the Foundation by The Policy Press (ISBN 1 86134 442 2, price £10.95)

---

# Experiences and expectations of people leaving paid work after 50

Increasing numbers of people are leaving employment before standard retirement ages, through a combination of factors such as choice, redundancy, health difficulties and increased care commitments. A new study by Helen Barnes, Jane Parry and Jane Lakey of the Policy Studies Institute examines the experiences of people in their fifties and sixties who have left paid work. The research looked at how people came to leave their jobs, how they had adjusted to life outside the labour market, and how they were spending their time in retirement. The study found that:

- Most of those interviewed continued to make identifiable contributions to society after leaving paid work. Activities included voluntary work, learning activities, domestic work, caring for family members (including elderly relatives and grandchildren), helping out friends and neighbours, and leisure pursuits.
- People's health, income and family circumstances were important in how they spent their time in retirement. Those who were better off found it easier to achieve a high level of participation.
- The ways in which people came to leave work were important in how well they adjusted to retirement. Those who freely chose to retire tended to have higher levels of income and more options open to them.
- Getting involved in activities outside the labour market had many benefits, including personal fulfilment, a sense of purpose, continued sociability and keeping physically and mentally alert.
- The older people interviewed felt that society should recognise their lifelong economic contributions. They were happy to continue to contribute, but felt that they should have more choice at this stage of their life about how they spent their time.
- In terms of policy implications, employment issues identified included the need for equality in retirement ages for men and women, and the abolition of compulsory retirement ages for those who want to continue working. The importance of a decent retirement income was also highlighted. The benefit system was seen as a key area for reform, including more proactive advice and information.

Published October 2002
(*Findings* reference number 022)

The full report, **Forging a new future: The experiences and expectations of people leaving paid work over 50** by Helen Barnes, Jane Parry and Jane Lakey, is published for the Foundation by The Policy Press (ISBN 1 86134 447 3, price £11.95).

# Public policy initiatives for older workers

Older workers' employment patterns and their relationship to population ageing and pension systems are of increasing concern to policy-makers. Philip Taylor at the University of Cambridge Interdisciplinary Research Centre on Ageing investigated how policy-making towards older workers is developing in several countries – Australia, Finland, Germany, Japan, the Netherlands and the USA. The project examined a broad range of policy areas: pension reform, equality, social security and labour-market policy. Key findings were that:

- The issue of the employment of older workers is rising up the policy agendas of the countries studied, although at different speeds.
- All the countries have policies targeting older workers, including:
    - removing previous incentives to early retirement;
    - encouraging later retirement and flexible retirement;
    - legislation to counter age discrimination;
    - awareness-raising campaigns among employers;
    - guidance and training programmes targeting older workers;
    - advice and guidance for employers;
    - employment placements;
    - support for labour-market intermediaries;
    - employment incentive schemes.
- Those countries which have ended mandatory retirement have not seen an immediate change in retirement patterns.
- Employment subsidies have had limited value, but have shown more potential when paid directly to employees.
- While consistently argued for, there is little evidence as yet of integration of public policies towards older workers, with the notable exception of Finland.
- The researcher concludes that there is a need for:
    - much greater integration of public policies towards older workers, with better links to other policy areas and greater recognition of the diverse needs of older workers;
    - greater emphasis on removing age barriers from existing initiatives, rather than developing special schemes for older workers;
    - better engagement with business.

Published December 2002
(*Findings* reference number D62)

---

The full report, **New policies for older workers** by Philip Taylor, is published for the Foundation by The Policy Press (ISBN 1 86134 463 5, price £13.95).

# Transitions from work to retirement: Developing a new social contract

Those over 50 now make up a significant proportion of the UK population. The changes facing this group are increasingly complex, affecting work, leisure, caring, volunteering and related activities. This report provides a detailed overview of the changes affecting people in their fifties and beyond.

The report brings together empirical and theoretical studies and includes a special analysis of the British Household Panel Survey. It also summarises important research from the US and Europe. The author provides a fresh perspective on middle age and makes recommendations on managing work and retirement policy. In particular, he challenges calls for raising retirement ages, arguing that paid employment is neither a feasible nor an attractive option for this group.

Published December 2002
(No *Findings* was published for this report)

The full report, **Transitions from work to retirement: Developing a new social contract** by Chris Phillipson, is published for the Foundation by The Policy Press (ISBN 1 86134 457 0, price £11.95).

# The role of flexible employment for older workers

Some of the increasing number of people leaving work before state pension age may benefit from more flexible jobs that bridge the gap between permanent full-time work and retirement. Stephen Lissenburgh and Deborah Smeaton of the Policy Studies Institute studied the role of such 'bridge jobs' in the lives of people leaving work between 50 and state pension age. Using national survey data, the research examined the characteristics and experiences of those leaving permanent jobs, factors associated with moving to temporary, part-time or self-employment and the qualities of these alternative forms of work.

- Leaving work tends to be a positive choice for workers with other advantages – including those (especially men) who have been with their present employer for longer, and are therefore more likely to have accumulated savings and pension entitlements, and those who have paid off their mortgages. People with health problems are also inclined to leave work early, especially low paid men; however, for them, 'early retirement' is more likely to have been due to an inability to stay in employment, rather than a positive choice.
- Similar divisions are apparent in entering flexible employment. Older workers from a more advantaged background are more likely to enter flexible employment rather than leave the workforce on departure from permanent full-time employment and are especially more likely to enter better quality flexible employment.
- The quality of flexible employment varies according to its type. Self-employment offers job quality most comparable to that enjoyed by permanent full-time employees. Temporary employment rates next in terms of job quality, although this is more the case for those on fixed-term contracts than casual workers or agency temps. Part-time employment offers the poorest job quality among the three types of flexible employment.
- Overall, women appear more successful than men in finding flexible jobs for positive reasons, but often find that these jobs are of poor quality.
- The research identified a need for policies to: help older people with health problems to remain in work; counter age discrimination; improve the skills of older workers; improve the financial incentives for older people to remain in work by offering them more generous tax credits and by increasing the National Minimum Wage; and provide better regulation of casual and agency temp work.

Published March 2003
(*Findings* reference number 343)

The full report, **Employment transitions of older workers: The role of flexible employment in maintaining labour market participation and promoting job quality** by Stephen Lissenburgh and Deborah Smeaton, is published for the Foundation by The Policy Press (ISBN 1 86134 475 9, price £13.95).

# Nurses over 50: Options, decisions and outcomes

Working patterns and retirement decisions of people over 50 have important implications for labour supply in an ageing workforce, nowhere more so than in a sector such as the National Health Service threatened with severe staff shortage. In this context, a study by researchers at the University of Hull examined the options and decisions taken by nurses over 50, and the outcomes in terms of their movement in and out of the NHS. They found that:

- The NHS has an ageing nursing workforce with more than 75,000 nurses aged over 55 and a further 71,000 aged 50–54. Almost 10,000 nurses retire each year. Many nurses over 50 ('older nurses') remain in nursing in the National Health Service (NHS) but growing numbers take early retirement. A small number return to nursing in their fifties.
- Despite government efforts to stem the loss of nurses from the NHS and to promote return to practice, older nurses lack clear advice, guidance and encouragement about the options they may take, when considering whether to retire or remain in nursing, and when deciding whether to return to NHS nursing from the outside.
- Attitudes to older nurses are sometimes ambivalent, sometimes apathetic and sometimes welcoming. Some older nurses reported ageist attitudes towards them by employers and their personnel departments, although employers also valued particular qualities that they associated with older nurses.
- Older nurses reported particular needs, but not much effort by employers to meet these. In particular:
  - They recognise their need for continuing professional development to help them keep up with a rapidly changing service, especially when returning after a career break. Yet opportunities are variable, and not geared towards the specific needs of older nurses.
  - Physical limitations or family caring responsibilities mean that some nurses would like to have less heavy duties or to reduce hours of work, but they report limited flexibility by employers in this regard.
  - Financial considerations may deter nurses from taking less demanding jobs, since this may compromise final pension entitlements.
  - Return to practice initiatives are not tailored towards the needs of older nurses.
- Overall, stakeholders in the nursing workforce, including senior NHS and nursing managers, human resources personnel, retirement organisations and trade unions, admit to a poor translation of government policy into practice in relation to older nurses in the NHS.

Published July 2003
(*Findings* reference number 793)

The full report, **Nurses over 50: Options, decisions and outcomes** by Roger Watson, Jill Manthorpe and JoyAnn Andrews, is published for the Foundation by The Policy Press (ISBN 1 86134 544 5, price £11.95).

# Informal care and work after 50

Many people in their fifties and sixties combine work with caring responsibilities for grandchildren, older relatives or their own children. Researchers at Thomas Coram Research Unit looked at how decisions about employment are influenced by the desire or need to provide informal care. The study, based on a survey, case studies and analysis of existing data, found that:

- People in their fifties represent a 'pivot' generation with both care and work roles:
    - two in three people between 50 and retirement age are in paid work;
    - by age 50, one in three people have grandchildren;
    - three in five 50-year-olds still have living parents;
    - nearly half those surveyed (who were working for, or recently retired from, two councils) had some caring responsibility.
- Despite increasing demand for elder care and childcare, changes in the population and in work patterns (for example if early retirement becomes harder) mean that fewer people will be available to provide informal care.
- Nearly as many men as women surveyed undertook informal care, but women's caregiving was more intensive.
- Few employees wanted to give up work in order to take on caring responsibilities. However, decisions about working were based on a combination of factors, including financial considerations, health, job satisfaction and stress, as well as caring responsibilities.
- Those who combined work and care often did so at personal cost such as tiredness, ill-health and lack of leisure. Most employees did all they could to avoid informal care having a negative impact on their paid work. However, opportunities for career advancement could be affected.
- Although some grandparents were prepared to give up work or reduce their hours to provide childcare for their grandchildren, there was a general reluctance to offer full-time care.
- The researchers conclude that without more resources to support carers, their contribution may not be sustainable. Flexible working hours, the opportunity to reduce hours or take a career break without financial penalties, and good-quality, affordable support for carers and care recipients would help employees to combine care and work.

Published October 2003
(*Findings* reference number 032)

---

The full report, **The pivot generation: Informal care and work after 50** by Ann Mooney and June Statham with Antonia Simon, is published for the Foundation by The Policy Press (ISBN 1 86134 402 3, price £11.95).

# The financial circumstances of early retirement

People leaving work before state pension age risk being poorer in retirement than if they had continued working. This qualitative study of 56 retired people in their fifties and early sixties profiled their experiences, decisions and attitudes before and after they stopped working. The study, by Sue Arthur of the National Centre for Social Research, found:

- People's experience of leaving work differed. Some had left willingly, others had had little choice. Some had left gradually, others abruptly. Some had planned the move, others had had it forced on them with little control over timing.
- These differences could have profound effects on people's experiences, including whether financial circumstances measured up to their expectations. Those with least choice and control tended to experience greatest difficulties.
- People in stronger financial and employment circumstances appeared to have more satisfactory experiences. Three factors in particular influenced people's experience: work history and skills; financial circumstances; and health and disability.
- On the whole, people in this study did not say that their financial situation was the dominant factor in deciding to move away from paid work. Instead, personal and work-related factors combined to influence motivations, with financial factors determining the viability of decisions.
- For people on the very lowest incomes, life was tough financially if they left work early but often little or no worse on benefits than when earning. However, early unplanned exit from a job for people on slightly higher earnings could result in extra hardship as it could seriously upset expectations for their financial future. People on average to high earnings tended to feel comfortable as long as they retired on at least half their earnings.
- People who had retired early generally found it hard to plan ahead for future, unknown, financial needs. Financial considerations did not seem at this stage to dominate how they felt about having left work, particularly in the case of those with health concerns, for whom not having the strain of working outweighed other factors.

Published December 2003
(*Findings* reference number D23)

The full report, **Money, choice and control: The financial circumstances of early retirement** by Sue Arthur, is published for the Foundation by The Policy Press (ISBN 1 86134 476 7, price £13.95).

# ■ Notes

1 More precisely, analysis of the Labour Force Survey looked at people between 50 and state pension age who were in full-time permanent jobs at a given interview, but not when interviewed a year later. At this later interview, 44 per cent were in some alternative form of paid work, 46 per cent had left the labour market and 10 per cent were not working but were looking for work (unemployed) (Lissenburgh and Smeaton 2003). See Chapter 5.

2 Hirsch (2000) reviewed existing evidence at the time that the Joseph Rowntree Foundation launched its 'Transitions After 50' research programme.

3 Aged 50–60 for women, 50–65 for men.

4 Author calculations based on Labour Force Survey statistics reported in the DWP Older people: statistical information booklet, Autumn 2002, and on National Statistics Population projections, 2000-based, London: The Stationery Office.

5 Interim findings of the University of Kent study, (Vickerstaff et al. 2003).

6 Author calculations based on DWP 'Older people: statistical information' booklet, Autumn 2002, and on National Statistics Incapacity Benefit and Severe Disablement Allowance Quarterly Summary Statistics, November 2002.

7 Private conversation with author.

8 For a fuller explanation of this proposal, see Donald Hirsch, 'Help the over-50s work part-time', New Statesman, 11 December 2000

9 Department for Work and Pensions, 2003, 'Income related benefits estimates of take-up in 2000/2001', shows that between 68 and 76 per cent of those entitled are claiming.

# Bibliography

Arthur, S. (2003) *Money, choice and control: The financial circumstances of early retirement*, Bristol: The Policy Press/Joseph Rowntree Foundation, *Transitions After 50 series*.

Atkinson, J., Evans C., Willison R., Lain, D. and Van Gent, M. (2003) *New Deal 50plus: Sustainability of employment*, London: DWP.

Audit Commission, (1997) *Retiring nature: Early retirement in local government*, London.

Bardasi, E. and Jenkins, S.P. (2002) *Income in later life: Work history matters*, Bristol: The Policy Press/Joseph Rowntree Foundation, *Transitions After 50 series*.

Bardasi, E., Jenkins, S.P. and Rigg, J.A. (2000) 'Retirement and the economic well-being of the elderly: A British perspective', working paper, University of Essex: Institute for Social and Economic Research.

Barnes, H., Parry J. and Lakey J. (2002) *Forging a new future: The experiences and expectations of people leaving paid work over 50*, Bristol: The Policy Press/Joseph Rowntree Foundation, *Transitions After 50 series*.

Beatty, C. and Fothergill, S. (1999) *The detached male workforce*, Sheffield: Sheffield Hallam University.

Cabinet Office, Performance and Innovation Unit (2000) *Winning the generation game: Improving opportunities for people aged 50–65 in work and community activity*, London: Stationery Office.

Campbell, N. (1999) 'The decline of employment among older people in Britain', CASE Paper 19, London: LSE/STICERD.

Department for Trade and Industry (2003) *Flexible working: The business case: 50 success stories*, London: The Stationery Office.

Department for Work and Pensions (2001) *Evaluation of the Code of Practice on age diversity in employment*, London: DWP.

Department for Work and Pensions (2002) *Simplicity, security and choice: Working and saving for retirement*, London: The Stationery Office.

Grattan, P. (2003) *Work after 60: Choice or necessity, burden or benefit?* London: Third Age Employment Network.

Gregg, P. and Wadsworth, J. (1998) *'Unemployment and non-employment: Unpacking economic activity'*, Economic Report 12, 6, London: Employment Policy Institute.

Hirsch, D. (ed.) (2000) *Life after 50: Issues for policy and research,* York: YPS/Joseph Rowntree Foundation.

Hornstein, Z. (ed.) (2001) *Outlawing age discrimination: Foreign lessons, UK choices,* Bristol: The Policy Press/Joseph Rowntree Foundation, *Transitions After 50 series.*

Jacobs, K. and Rein, M. (1994) *'Early retirement: Stability, reversal, or redefinition',* in F. Naschold and B de Vroom (eds) Regulating employment and welfare, Berlin: De Gruyter, 17.

Learning and Skills Council (2001) *Strategic framework to 2004 – Corporate plan,* Coventry: LSC.

Lissenburgh, S. and Smeaton, D. (2003) *Employment transitions of older workers: The role of flexible employment in maintaining labour market participation and promoting job quality,* Bristol: The Policy Press/Joseph Rowntree Foundation, *Transitions After 50 series.*

McKay, S. and Middleton, S. (1998) *Characteristics of older workers: Secondary analysis of the family and working lives Survey,* DfEE RR45, London: The Stationery Office.

Meadows, P. (2002) *Early retirement and income in later life,* Bristol: The Policy Press/Joseph Rowntree Foundation, *Transitions After 50 series.*

Meghir, C. and Whitehouse, E. (1997) 'Labour market transitions and retirement of men in the UK', Journal of Econometrics, 79, 327-54.

Mooney, A. and Statham, J. (2002) *The pivot generation: Informal care and work after 50,* Bristol: The Policy Press/Joseph Rowntree Foundation, *Transitions After 50 series.*

Phillipson, C. (2002) *Transitions from work to retirement: Developing a new social contract,* Bristol: The Policy Press/Joseph Rowntree Foundation, *Transitions After 50 series.*

Power, Maria (forthcoming 2004) *Initiatives to help older people to volunteer* (provisional title), Bristol: The Policy Press/Joseph Rowntree Foundation, *Transitions after 50 series.*

Tanner, S. (1997) 'Dynamics of retirement behaviour', in R. Disney, E. Grundy and P. Johnson (eds) Dynamics of retirement: Analyses of the retirement surveys, London: Department for Social Security.

Taylor, P. (2002) *New policies for older workers,* Bristol: The Policy Press/Joseph Rowntree Foundation, *Transitions After 50 series.*

Tuchman, B (1985) *March of folly: From Troy to Vietnam,* London: Abacus.

Vickerstaff, S., Cox, J. and Keen, L. (2003) 'Employers and the management of retirement', *Social Policy and Administration, 37* (3), 271–87.

Vickerstaff, S., Baldock, J. and Cox, J. (forthcoming 2004) *Impact of employers' policies and practice on the process of retirement* (provisional title), Bristol: The Policy Press/Joseph Rowntree Foundation, *Transitions After 50 series.*

Watson, R., Manthorpe, J. and Andrews, J. (2003) *Nurses over 50: Options, decisions and outcomes,* Bristol: The Policy Press/Joseph Rowntree Foundation, *Transitions After 50 series.*